# प्रज्ञा

**Mīra Manek** is a writer, cook and wellness expert with a passion for yoga and Ayurveda. She was born and brought up in London, has lived in Uganda and Dubai and has travelled extensively in India. Growing up speaking Gujarati, learning Sanskrit at school and exploring India while she travelled to attend Ram Kathas (nine-day spiritual events) inspired Mīra's passion for philosophy and spirituality. She first started visiting Ayurvedic retreats and spas twenty years ago in a quest to rejuvenate, detox and learn yoga. Since moving back to London five years ago, Mīra has been hosting supper clubs and retreats and has also launched her own café, Chai by Mira, inside Triyoga Soho. Mīra published her first cookbook in 2017, *Saffron Soul,* inspired by the flavours of her mother's and grandmother's vegetarian food of the Gujarat region. Follow her journey, events and retreats on Instagram: @miramanek.

www.miramanek.com

# MĪRA MANEK

# PRAJÑĀ

Ayurvedic rituals for happiness

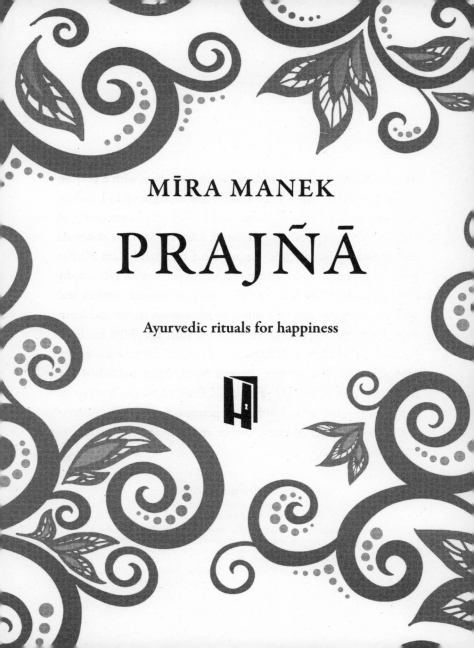

First published in 2019 by HEADLINE HOME
An imprint of HEADLINE PUBLISHING GROUP

1

Cataloguing in Publication Data is available from the British Library

ISBN 978 1 4722 6770 2

Illustrations by Ruth Craddock

Designed and typeset by EM&EN
Printed and bound in Great Britain by Clays Ltd, Elcograf S.p.A.

Headline's policy is to use papers that are natural, renewable and recyclable
products and made from wood grown in sustainable forests. The logging and
manufacturing processes are expected to conform to the environmental
regulations of the country of origin.

HEADLINE PUBLISHING GROUP
An Hachette UK Company
Carmelite House
50 Victoria Embankment
London
EC4Y 0DZ
www.headline.co.uk
www.hachette.co.uk

The information and advice contained in this book are intended as a general
guide. It is not intended as and should not be relied upon as medical advice.
The publisher and author are not responsible for any specific health needs
that may require medical supervision. If you have underlying health problems,
you should contact a qualified medical professional.

*Thank you,*

*India, my motherland;*

*my parents and grandparents, for instilling and infusing our life with culture and meaningful rituals;*

*my school St. James, for imparting the Sanskrit language, the key to the scriptures;*

*thank you to my spiritual teacher Morari Bapu for his kathas, his wisdom and some of the most magical experiences of my life;*

*to Alan Watts, whose recordings, voice and philosophy I never tire of, always with sprinkles of humour;*

*a deep gratitude to loneliness for making me find myself;*

*yoga and sunshine for picking me up;*

*and the incredible yoga teachers I've learnt from*

*. . . and finally to London, my home, for being so open, so embracing and forever inspiring.*

# Contents

# INTRODUCTION

As far back as I can remember, I woke up each day to the classical sounds of morning *ragas* and sandalwood incense *(agarbatti)* floating through the house. It was rhythm and clockwork. The first thing my father did.

During my years living abroad in my twenties, I would often remember those two things when my eyes opened. Sometimes I would light *agarbatti*, but I didn't have any means of playing the *ragas*. At the time, I don't think I was bothered about waking up to silence. It is only now, when I look back, that I remember the silence becoming deafening, particularly during those days when my marriage was falling apart and I was trying to keep afloat in the depths of loneliness.

I realize now that small rituals can uplift the soul, that waking up to a positive sound or something that makes us smile, even if only internally, spreads positivity and over time that positivity becomes a part of our make-up, influencing our thoughts, and elevating our mood. The *ragas* and the *agarbatti* became symbolic only once I felt their absence. And this is the beauty of rituals. Once they are a part of our life, they just happen.

I grew up practising little things, and they became habits, they became my rituals. Rituals can be practised daily, such as taking deep breaths, or seasonally, like having ginger and turmeric in the colder months. Just like we brush our teeth or get a morning coffee on our way to work, there are certain rituals that provide stability through different times in life.

Rituals are beautiful practices that keep us in tune with ourselves. They need no routine or pattern, nor are they bound by time. They keep us in harmony with the seasons, they provide purpose, they ground us. You can pick and choose, find your own set of rituals to embed in daily life, and so create your own language, something that you'll always revert to, rather like a mother tongue. The whole purpose of this book is for you to choose what you can do and want to do, and what works for you.

Taking a moment to say thank you, a breathing exercise or yoga, a pause before a meeting, remembering to chew, sipping hot lemon water. You can curate your own playlist of practices, which you can edit and add to. Spending five minutes in silence first thing in the morning, going inward or doing breathing exercises that energize and detox you, can set the tone for the day.

I think of the rituals in this book as a toolkit for life, a toolkit that is founded on Indian and Ayurvedic principles. In this book, I have taken practices that have meaning in my life, bolstered them, added other rituals, and woven these together with threads of spirituality and strands of philosophy. From this, you can create your own personal toolbox, a package of resilience for life's lows, a shield from dipping further and a way to bounce back.

The rituals in this book can give you a spring in your step in the morning, increase your resilience during the day and calm and de-stress you when you get home in the evening. Pick from uplifting affirmations, understand the power of mantras, explore the depth of your breath and scroll through a list of ancient remedies for everything from bloating to soothing a headache. Throughout the book there are recipes for all times of the day, including a simple yet detailed prep guide for your weekday lunches, and information on how to eat according to Ayurveda.

These rituals are also a way to keep you connected to your own self, to discover yourself, to reconnect with all the magic, fascination and energy you were born with. They are practices that help you live with the glow of wellbeing and health, but also with awareness and presence.

We all go through times of darkness and light of differing intensities, for life is an incredible balancing act. But how do we cope with and emerge from the darkness, how do we deal with the day-to-day angst of being in an unhappy state when we're living it and how do we unravel ourselves from it and regain clarity and happiness?

Ayurveda acknowledges the mind-body-spirit connection; life wisdom and philosophy are fully entwined with our physical wellbeing. Living with stress and in a state of fear will have an impact on both our mental and physical health and affect our longevity, and so learning from the ancient wisdom found in Indian philosophy – whether it's something as simple as mindfulness or the concept of the soul and the inner Self – grounds us with strength, roots us with an understanding of the meaning of life and gives us the capacity to deal with life situations.

You never really know how you're going to deal with a tragedy – a death, a break up or any difficult circumstance – until it presents itself to you, sometimes very suddenly. This is where your daily practices, rituals of happiness, can become your toolbox of survival, enabling you to surf any giant wave and keep afloat, breathing through it, going with it and not against it, and arriving the other side hopefully with more grace, perhaps a little disheveled but certainly transformed. It can be hard to keep your head above water when you're in the depths of a difficult time, but eventually your tragedy has the potential to become your ultimate remedy. Looking inside, searching within and just surviving can be enough sometimes. We need to give room for that strength to grow. It is often the most painful times of our life that allow the seed of our identity to blossom. Meditation, sitting still, listening to our own thoughts, observing emotions passing through us, dipping into memories but coming back to the present moment, all of these things reconnect us to our own identity, what we are beneath the layers of connections with others, the titles afforded by our careers and the definition of ourselves through the eyes of our communities.

Take those things that call to you and create a habit, let them become a part of your life. Whether on the happier days or the stressful days, this is your own set of keys to connect within, to heal yourself and to live with more zest.

# MY JOURNEY

I grew up in a very traditional and large Indian family. Gujarati was my first language, we wore *salwars* and *saris* for festivals and family occasions, we took a day off school on our New Year's Day, danced almost every night during the nine-day festival of Navratri and learned *rangolis* (a traditional art form that uses coloured rice, sand or petals to create patterns on the ground during festivals) from our grandfather on Diwali. Significant life occasions were and still are filled with beautiful ceremonies, from holding a *chhathi* on the sixth day after a baby is born, a welcoming, a writing of destiny, to *balmuwara*, the shaving of the hair at the age of one, and *khoro* which is rather like a baby shower. I also did a lot of travelling around India very early on, mostly to attend the spiritual recitals of Ram Katha in the villages and cities with my spiritual teacher Morari Bapu and to discover parts of this colourful country in between. My experiences were fascinating and varied, from learning yoga for the very first time from 85-year-old Daya Vyas, known as 'yoga mother', who lived in Jaipur, to working with a grassroots non-profit organisation called Manav Sadhna at Gandhi Ashram in Ahmedabad, which works with different slum communities and children, to staying in an Ayurvedic resort in South India where I spent my 18th birthday, alone! I cannot recall how this transpired exactly, but my father always found a new Ayurvedic resort for me to visit during my travels around India, everywhere from Kerala to Calcutta. At that time, I had put on weight and developed acne, so I was eager to immerse myself in Ayurvedic practices to cleanse and purify the body, even though I didn't quite understand what the oils and massages were doing or why the food was so healing.

From around this time, my late teens, my life rolled into a sporadic series of study and work and travel, and the periods of travel extended as I grew older. Even when I was married, I lived between Dubai and Uganda, travelling incessantly as a travel journalist, a career that I thought worked well with my husband's peripetatic life. This meant that everything about my life became as chaotic as it was once balanced. I loved those years, I wore the badge of being a free spirit with such pride and joy, but I also battled with my health, my emotions and later on my marriage.

I met an Ayurvedic practitioner, a *vaidya*, when I was married and living in Dubai. He told me everything about my physical issues, my life and history from feeling my pulse and he was correct about everything. At the end, he added with a smile and slight hesitation, 'Mīra, there is no happiness pulse. I can't feel any happiness.' I didn't think I was entirely unhappy, but I was simply living life and coping with feeling alone in my marriage with a sense of acceptance. I was *doing* but not *feeling*. Soon the numbness developed or rather collapsed into depression, anger and rage.

It's only now, years later, that I understand that pulse, the meaning of inner happiness. It takes time to resuscitate the pulse of life, and in the process of reawakening there might unfold a transformation, an unfurling of true self. It is this pulse that gives life to our soul, provides a reason to live and is the essence of connection.

I never knew there was so much in my life to be undone: the way I was conditioned, the way I saw myself, the way I lived in my head. These issues were connected to how I perceived my body and my idea or ideal of beauty. Soul searching came hand in hand with regaining balance and healthfulness.

Transformation is rather like childbirth. The painful moments of labour are so hard to bear that all you want is to stop the agony, but you have to see it through, and at the end, you gaze upon this beautiful child. In the same way, at your absolute lowest point, you can feel as though you're drowning, but there is wisdom in these deepest emotions, and if you let them complete their work, you might discover a miraculous transformation, a rebirth of your strength, an outburst of all that joy that was contained and suppressed deep within.

It is often emotional breakdown that leads to finding our purpose and making change. The rituals of practising yoga, looking inward, using our breath and being still help us not only gain clarity of thought, mind and heart, but also equip us with ready tools to use when we find ourselves in a state of crisis. In high-stress situations, we will be able to turn those tools into weapons to shield us, to help us accept the situation and understand that pain is a part of the journey, but also to battle through it so that we can emerge from it quicker and with a sense of growth.

# PRAJÑĀ

*Prajñā* is a Sanskrit word meaning ultimate wisdom. It is made of two parts, *pra* meaning 'before' or 'supreme' and *jñā* which means 'knowledge' or 'consciousness'. It is translated as intuitive wisdom, root knowledge and deep understanding. *Prajñā* is accessed from stillness, akin to the concept of *shunyata*, nothingness, where thoughts and events of the mind are observed and noted without any connection to our story or experience, without connecting a past occurrence with the present moment, without any presuppositions. Just living in the now. Being mindful, being right here, right now, moves us closer to *prajñā*.

The concept of *prajñā*, rather like in Zen philosophy, is the ability to be spontaneous and respond with playfulness to life's events as they pop up with surprise like hiccoughs. It doesn't mean sitting silent and becoming numb to life; rather, it is having all those emotional human responses but with a sense of inner jest, being in it yet simultaneously being the observer, a secret play with the Self.

It is echoed in the concept of *mushin* in Zen Buddhism. *Mushin* translates as 'mind without mind' or mindlessness, a mind that is in fact entirely present, a mind free from worry, free from anger and fear, a mind that is truly mind-ful. It is the realization that we do not need to strive for *moksha*, liberation from the cycle of life and rebirth, but that living in the bliss of this moment, the present, living with awareness, this itself is liberation, ultimate freedom. But spiritual awakening should not afford a sense of superiority. It is simply a chosen path that provides a new lens with which to view this world and our existence in it.

Mindfulness is a wonderful and accessible concept that has become popular because our lives have moved so far away from the present moment and we are now understanding the impact of that absence. The roots of this concept lie in the spiritual realms of all religions. *Prajñā* is the realization of this, being present in all that we do, playing the game of life with less seriousness, accessing higher consciousness through a still mind and finding happiness in the *shunyata* – the vast expanse or emptiness – of life.

Ayurveda, the wellbeing toolbox for life, is what opens our eyes and lets us access *prajñā*. Being still, observing the breath and practising rituals that unlock the chakras (energy points) and channels in our body so that our *prana*, our vital energy, can flow freely, gives space for the mind to enter realms of higher consciousness. Once you start deepening the breath, you start observing the breath and then observing the body, allowing you in turn to experience the body as something other than the Self, and understanding your spiritual experience on this earth. This is *prajñā*.

Living with this understanding, the realization of this world as *maya*, magic or illusion, living with awareness of our experience of life rather than the reality of life, allows us to be in a state of joy, or *ananda*. This joy comes from adding a sprinkle of humour to life, from taking life less seriously and from understanding that the highs and the lows are both an essential part of the equation.

Understanding that this life is an experience, and being a part of it, yet able to step away and observe it, gives us better insight and perspective. It's like having a cloud removed from our mind and seeing the blue sky. The colour and intensity of emotion is still alive, but with wisdom comes a sense of freedom, a lack of fear and a passion for living.

*Prajñā* is higher wisdom, spiritual insight and the truth of awakening. It is not the knowledge of God or religion, it is not intellect, nor is it being pious and praying, though it could encompass all of these.

# AYURVEDA

Ayurveda, a Sanskrit word meaning the knowledge, science or scripture of life, is the basis of traditional holistic medicine in India. The teachings of this scripture are as relevant today as they were thousands of years ago. Ayurveda is one of the world's oldest medical systems. It was developed by ancient seers, sages and natural scientists based on the premise that humans come from nature and from the universe, therefore our bodily rhythms and wellbeing are intrinsically linked to nature.

At the heart of Ayurveda is balance and living in tune with nature. *When* you eat – such as having your largest meal at lunchtime when the sun is at its strongest and therefore your digestive fire or *agni* is also at its strongest – is just as important as *what* you eat and *how much* you eat. Movement and yoga go hand in hand with food, and keeping the mind at ease and not allowing for stress is an essential part of the package. Thus, it is a lifestyle comprising of and connecting the elements of mind, body and spirit, a lifestyle that is wholesome, pure and nourishing, eating foods that are light, fuelled with energy and *prana*, for it is said in the ancient scripture of The Upanishads that food is Brahman, the higher consciousness, the true Self, the Divine.

Ayurveda is full of practices and guides that we can apply to our daily life, from how to ensure our digestion is functioning well to how to eat for our own body composition and why that might differ from someone else. It is practical science intertwined with philosophy. Its overarching principle is to live a more sattvic life by instilling daily rituals to bring about balance, prevent disease and promote longevity – all of which create and fuel happiness.

*Doshas* **and humors** ❧ Ayurvedic medicine is based on balance and harmony. Our wellness and happiness depend on living in harmony with our environment and achieving an internal balance between opposing forces or energies. First there are the three fundamental bodily energies, or *doshas*. These are *vata*, which is characterized by the mobile nature of wind energy; *pitta*, which embodies transformative fire energy; and *kapha*, which reflects the binding nature of water energy. We are made up of these *doshas* and the balance of the three in our body determine our physical and emotional constitution. It is this that determines what we should and should not be eating, how our energy levels rise and fall throughout the day and change according to the season. An Ayurvedic practitioner or *vaidya* can determine this accurately, assess which elements are in balance and which are out, and then diagnose according to this. By implementing certain practices and changes, we can live in accordance with our *doshas* and keep the *doshas* in balance. This balance, in Ayurveda, is the key to good health.

This is similar to the concept of humors in Greek medicine, which was developed by Hippocrates. The humors were the bodily fluids – blood, phlegm, yellow bile and black bile – that were believed to make up the body's constitution. Temperament was associated with the humors – sanguine, choleric, melancholic and phlegmatic. Rather like the *doshas*, good health is the state in which these constituents are in the correct proportion and well balanced.

**Essence and quality** ❧ In addition to the *doshas*, which form our physiological constitution, there are three overarching qualities, known as *gunas*, that determine our psychological character but are also present in our actions, our food and habits. These are *sattva* (which means purity and equilibrium), *rajas* (energetic activity) and *tamas* (inertia), and they relate to everything from our levels of consciousness and our personalities to the energy present in the food we eat and how it makes us feel. Our bodies and all that we do are a complex interplay of all three *gunas*, but being aware of these, we try to imbibe a more sattvic and rajasic quality of living. This also relates to food: sattvic foods are foods that are pure, fresh and lightly seasoned, that give us positive energy and bring about calmness. Rajasic foods are strong in flavour – they could be spicy, sweet or stimulating, firing the belly with power, ambition and high energy. Lastly, foods that are tamasic in quality can include meats, alcohol and deep-fried foods. Tamasic foods are conducive to laziness, lethargy, irritability and other such qualities. Essentially, the food we eat is our life and energy source, it feeds our thoughts and can change our being.

**Chakras** ❧ The word chakra translates as wheel or disc. In our body, there are seven main chakras, or wheels of energy and light, which align from the base of the spine through to the crown of the head. The invisible energy or life force called *prana* flows through these centres of energy. When the chakras are aligned and open, the *prana* flows freely through them and there is balance in the body. Both physical and emotional issues can cause blockages in the chakras and breathwork, yoga and meditation can all help unblock these energy centres and help regain balance.

The First Chakra is the *Muladhara* or Root Chakra, located at the base of the spine. This is the chakra of stability and security, encompassing the first three vertebrae, the bladder and colon.

The Second Chakra is the *Svadhisthana* or Sacral Chakra, located above the pubic bone, below the navel, representing our creativity and sexual centre.

The Third Chakra is the *Manipura* or Solar Plexus Chakra located in the upper abdomen. This is our source of confidence and personal power.

The Fourth Chakra is the *Anahata* or Heart Chakra, located at the centre of the chest just above the heart, uniting the lower chakras of matter and the upper chakras of spirit. It serves as a bridge between our body, mind, emotions, and spirit. This is the chakra of love and joy.

The Fifth Chakra is *Vishuddha* or Throat Chakra, located in the area of the throat, emcompassing the neck, thyroid, jaw, mouth and tongue. This is our source of communication, verbal expression and speaking our truth.

The Sixth Chakra is the *Ajna* or Third Eye Chakra, located between the eyebrows. This is our centre of intuition and wisdom.

The Seventh Chakra is the *Sahaswara* or Crown Chakra, located at the crown (the very top) of the head. This is the chakra of enlightenment, spiritual connection and bliss, and is our connection to the divine.

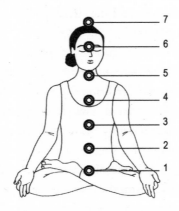

**Connecting to nature** ✋ Our bodies and minds are instinctively attuned to nature. We seem to have lost that over time through our busy lives with its myriad of distractions, diversions and temptations. Ayurveda is a way to find this connection again, a back-to-basics approach to life at the centre of which is self-awareness. The practice of meditation is to bring about this very thing – a sense of self, understanding the inner voice, listening to our body, connecting with nature. And being present is key to this, thus we find ourselves at the origin of mindfulness.

According to Ayurveda, humans came from nature and so we must find a way to bridge the gap between the ancient and modern ways of living, a way to connect with our roots and, like a tree, grow those roots and be stable in ourselves, so that we stand tall and remain grounded through the intense storms and blistering sunshine of life. The answer to health and healing is in the balance of the senses and the elements, both in our body and mind and in the universe.

**The energy source, *prana*, *chi* or *pneuma*** ∾ One of the key features that Ayurveda, Traditional Chinese Medicine (TCM) and Ancient Greek medicine have in common, despite having been developed independently in different parts of the world, is the acknowledgement of a source of energy, the vital energy – *prana* (Ayurveda), *chi* (Chinese) or *pneuma* (Greek) – that travels through the body and forms the base of all kinetic functions in our body. This energy flows through the energy centres called *nadis* (in the Indian system) or *meridians* (Chinese system). It is blockages in these centres that stop the energy from flowing around the body and are the cause of low energy, illness and disease.

The healing systems of acupuncture, acupressure, massage and yoga are founded on the principles of *prana* or *chi*; they help to remove energy blockages and thus free the movement of energy through the energy pathways. This is also where the *chakras* come into play. The flow of energy or *prana* is the energy of the physical body, the subtle body and the causal body, flowing through the 350,000 *nadis*. These *nadis* connect at points of intensity called *nadichakras*.

Often times, emotions and trauma get stuck and stored in different places in our bodies. The Chinese believe that anger, for example, is stored in the liver, fear in the kidneys and sadness in the lungs. Each emotion has its residential home. This is sometimes why your body might ache persistently in a specific area and you might need regular massage, after which, at some point, it will hopefully pass. This is also why bodywork, such as acupuncture, marma massage or reflexology, with someone who really understands the body and who understands the mind-body connection, can be more transformative than a massage, which will certainly give temporary relief but might not work on the root cause of the whole issue.

*Agni*, the digestive fire   In India, during spiritual and Vedic rituals, a *havan*, a *yagna*, or spiritual fire is made and *ahuti* or oblations are offered into the fire while chanting mantras. The fire absorbs and takes what it needs in order to burn brighter and eliminates the rest. In the same way, our digestive fire is kindled with cooked foods, our body assimilates the nutrients it needs and eliminates what it does not need. Eating cooked foods, drinking warm to hot water, fasting between meals and practising yoga and *pranayama* (see page 40) all help to stimulate the *agni*. Having a good digestive system, a fire that is well fed, means we produce a biochemical or subtle force called *ojas*. This is the fruit of our digestion, our inner glow radiating externally, the product of free-flowing prana, the essence of harmony in our body and mind.

**Nourishment and food** ✌ The sattvic food mentioned above is food that is primarily vegetarian, freshly cooked and hot, food that is easy to digest (cooking foods increases their digestibility) and food that is not overly spiced or oily. The body exists because of food, and the right diet can prevent disease and can help to heal the body and mind. Food is our source of energy and it has a life-force which is lost in artificial or fast food. Connecting with nature through the process of cooking, understanding what we are eating and putting good thoughts into our food is conducive to the sattvic way of living, as is eating in the proper amounts and on an empty stomach. Indian food originates in Ayurvedic cooking; some of this has been lost in translation over the years as modern Indian cooking is characterized by excess oil and spice, but the flavours in this more basic style of cooking are subtle, varied and easy to create. Each spice has an array of health benefits and different combinations of spices bring about very different flavours, ensuring variety and making food more interesting.

**Covering all tastes** ❧ In Ayurveda, each of the six tastes – salty, sour, sweet, bitter, pungent and astringent – should be covered in a meal. Each taste has an effect on the *doshas* and can be used to balance the *dosha* in our body that is most imbalanced. A *vata* body type is balanced by salt, sour and sweet; *pitta* is balanced by bitter, sweet and astringent; and *kapha* by pungent, bitter and astringent. Incorporating each taste in a meal allows us to feel satisfied and so prevent cravings after the meal and prevent snacking for the next few hours. This is one of the crucial rules of Ayurveda: not to eat the next meal until the previous meal is completely digested, allowing the digestive fire to be kept alive. According to Ayurveda, we should eat according to our body types, and if we are really in tune with our bodies, this should be akin to intuitive eating, understanding what our body needs and being guided by that. To find out more about your *dosha* and body type, it is best to see an Ayurvedic practitioner (see page 245).

**A brief history** ❧ For many years, the information we now know as Ayurveda was passed on verbally through the verses of the Vedas, the earliest body of Indian scripture. It was then recorded in the various Vedas from the *Rig Veda* (approximately 4,500 years old) and then the *Atharva Veda* (3,200 years ago), describing the herbs and medicines of ancient India in hymn form. After this, the knowledge contained in these texts was further expounded in the *Charaka Samhita* in Punjab and then the *Susruta Samhita* in Benares written by Ayurvedic teachers Charaka and Susruta respectively. Ayurveda then thrived during the reign of King Ashoka, who renounced violence when he became a Buddhist, and Ayurveda became the foundation for the Tibetan Buddhist system of healing and also influenced parts of Chinese medicine. During the Muslim invasion of India in 1100 and 1200AD, Ayurveda was replaced by the system of healing called Unani founded by Hippocrates in Greece, which is still in existence today, but both are ancient systems of medicine that believe in healing with plants and the importance of diet and food, both are based on the idea of the constitution, and both recognize the connection of the physical with the spiritual, emotional and mental. It is only when the British Raj started that Ayurveda was suppressed. The British closed all Ayurvedic colleges in India in 1833, and only Western Medicine was to be practised. After the independence of India, Ayurvedic schools and pharmacies arose again, with government support. Which brings us to now, an age in which we see the revival of this ancient science. Ayurveda is more popular than ever before . . . and not just in India but all over the world.

**Supplements** ❧ Ever since I fractured two bones in my feet at separate times a few years apart, once while running and the second time dancing, I've been much more careful about what I eat and the supplements I take. It might not have been my diet that caused these injuries, but it is possible that the impact might have been less serious, or that it could have resulted in a sprained ankle rather than a full fracture, if my bones were stronger.

Yes, in an ideal world, we should be able to get everything we need from our food and diet, but we are living in a time where our food doesn't usually come directly from the ground. Depending on the vegetable or fruit, its storage time could be anywhere from 1 week to 12 months. There is therefore inevitably a depletion of nutrients (and also of the *prana* in these fresh foods, according to Ayurveda), which is why it can be difficult to get all the nutrients that our bodies and minds need solely from our food sources. A vegetable that is nutrient-rich may have lost some, even most, of its nutrients by the time we eat it a few weeks or months after it was plucked from the soil. Furthermore, for vegetarians or vegans, it is a little more difficult to obtain enough of certain vitamins and minerals from plant sources. And therefore, supplements can aid all diets.

Vitamin D deficiency, for example, can lead to a loss of bone density and neurological disorders such as depression, among other things. Being low in iron, more common for vegetarians, can cause anaemia and extreme tiredness. If you're getting muscle cramps and you're not able to sleep properly, this could be an indication of magnesium deficiency. Detecting certain deficiencies such as magnesium can be difficult as it is not a part of routine blood work and yet it is such a vital mineral. It is therefore important to understand what the symptoms of a vitamin or mineral insufficiency are, what foods contain the nutrients that we need and to take certain supplements. It is also important to understand nutrient synergies; for example, vitamin D and vitamin

K2 (found in eggs, butter and ghee) work together to maintain control over calcium levels in the body. And it is just as important to realize how nutrients can be depleted, for example alcohol and carbonated drinks reduce magnesium in the body through their high phosphate and sugar content and their diuretic properties. Everything is linked, and this is why it is so important to have a balanced diet and not to cut out whole food groups unless there is an allergy.

Ayurveda is all about creating balance in the body and while deficiencies in vitamins may not have been a concern in the time when Ayurveda was born, we now have access to a wealth of information, brilliant nutritionists and advanced doctors, along-side both the ancient Indian and Chinese systems of medicine. So we can still adopt Ayurveda and ancient practices, but we can adapt and bolster this timeless science with new research. As one Chinese doctor told me, there's heaps of gold dust and heaps of junk – you've just got to find the gold and what works for you.

### Finding happiness in yoga

India always beckons me. It's where I feel alive. The electric energy on the streets of Mumbai, riding through the dusty heat in a rickshaw, that smell of Bombay sandwiches being made on one side of the road and sweet masala chai on the other; homemade, frothy, steaming *kichri kadhi* (a blend of rice and dal), just like my grandmother's; speaking in Gujarati, sweet, raw and so humorous; the overnight train journeys and being woken by the chaiwalla running up and down the platform shouting 'chai' at the top of his voice; admiring age-old trees with magnificent intertwined branches; the markets of Delhi in blistering heat; the smell of *agarbatti*, incense, burning in the temples and bells chiming; and then up north the hills of Rishikesh, the immense flow of the Ganga, and the spellbinding stillness of the Himalayas. It is these experiences, awakening every sense in a single moment, and the incredible contrasts that colour India, that draw me back time and time again, and make me realize how much of an Indian soul I really am.

While I have visited India for as long as I can remember, it is only when my life began to fall apart that I came to regard India as my best friend. During years of struggling through the end of a lonely marriage and then a long divorce, I started coming back to India more frequently and found yoga. Yoga House in Mumbai became my newfound haven when I was there, where I practised yoga and then ate their healing Ayurvedic food while reading and writing. Slowly, during that time, I began resolving my issues with food, realising why I needed to eat nourishing food simply because it felt better and why I should return to the Gujarati home-cooked food I had grown up eating, both Ayurvedic and sattvic, and I found a new direction in life.

# LIFE AND RITUALS IN INDIA

There is a sense of ritual, absorption and purpose in the homes and on the streets of India. As a young girl, my grandmother would churn *chaas* buttermilk with her friend, an hour-long process requiring full body movement and turning of hips. She carried and balanced pots of water on her head and hip – functional ways to exercise the body.

On the streets of Mumbai, I'll watch men slurping their shot of chai on their way to work, immersed in the cup, inhaling as they slowly take sips and wait for the sweet, spicy, strong and piping hot energy to seep into their blood.

From the villages to the cities, short afternoon siestas – *aram* – are an essential part of the day, a necessary rest after a full meal, but also to stay in the cool indoors when the sun is at its peak. I often see rickshawallas and taxi drivers snoozing in reclined car seats in the afternoon heat.

*Aarti* time, worship, much like the call to prayer, happens at dawn and at dusk in temples and often in people's homes. A candle is lit on a plate, and devotion expressed through song and prayer as the small fire or candle is moved in a clockwise motion facing the deity.

The reasons for certain rituals might not be articulated or

understood, but there is a reason why a *sathiya* or swastika symbol at the entrance of a home is made using red kumkum powder, or why a bindi is worn on the forehead of women and tilak, usually made with pure sandalwood paste, on the forehead of holy men, to activate the third eye. There is a reason why certain heavier grains like millet are eaten in the winter to keep you warm, energetic and full and why the drink chaas or lassi is best in the summer, to cool the body.

There are reasons for the beautiful ancient rituals of every culture and civilization, rituals that are purposeful and timeless, but may seem impractical or lacking purpose in our modern lives and are thus being forgotten. Beaded malas have gained popularity in the West through the resurgence of yoga; the power of chanting a mantra is now a concept that many know and practice, but in India, these meaningful practices started slipping away from one generation to the next a while ago. We grew up having turmeric stirred into hot milk as a medicinal drink if we had a cold or as a winter remedy, but we would be forced to drink it rather than actually enjoy it. Now, some two or three decades later, I would choose to have it anytime of day and I serve it in my own café, something that seems so normal now and yet a few years ago, I would have been very surprised to find a turmeric latte on the menu!

Death is something that we fear, something that we don't mention, even in my own family, yet in some lineages in India, death is a *mahotsav*, a celebration of life, with a music-filled evening that starts with a procession to the temple followed by a feast and music until the early hours of the morning. This does not happen all over India, but it is wonderful to experience this sense of revelling in a person's life and sending their soul off with joy, rather than mourning our loss of their human body.

In some ways, the West has given new meaning to and understanding of Ayurvedic practices. When my sister was breastfeeding, our mother insisted that she ate specific foods, such as dill curry, raab (see page 180) and katlu homemade energy squares (containing over 30 ingredients including jaggery, ghee and *goondh* edible gum). And yet our mother couldn't explain the exact reason, although she knew they were good for producing milk, healing the body and for the digestion of both mother and baby. There is so much to be learned from this ingrained wisdom that our parents and grandparents have locked in their memories, something that comes so naturally to them but that we're only now discovering and realizing the benefits of.

On the other hand, it is also worth challenging and questioning certain traditions, which might be practised out of fear and ancient practicality – such as a woman not being able to enter the temple area of one's own home or attend a ceremony or prayer if she is on her menstrual cycle. In fact, even though there is no word in Gujarati for period, you say *chokkhai nathi*: 'She is not clean or pure', which itself projects a sense of shame. Furthermore, it is entirely forbidden for a woman on her period to attend the nine-day dance festival of Navratri, but when you consider the fact that this festival is celebrating Goddess Amba Maa, who represents *shakti*, the divine female energy, and that the word for the dance is 'garba', which itself means womb, it seems entirely ludicrous. The only reason I can think of is that Ayurveda considers the menstrual cycle as a chance for a woman's body to purify and reset, and that therefore this is a time for a woman to rest and not work or exercise or dance – perhaps this practical reason that's rooted in wellbeing has adopted a religious meaning.

It is useful, even necessary, to look at these ancient health systems, as well as some of the traditions that we practise, from a modern viewpoint and from a point of understanding and reasoning. We can, for example, understand how the terminology of *chokkhai nathi* came about years ago in the villages of India when sanitary towels were not available, but this is something that now must clearly change. Any traditions or rituals that we have in our lives must work for us; this is not to disregard their worth and value, but to question them and practise with purpose.

# PART ONE

# MORNING

There are some days when we wake up feeling happy and at ease, and others with a pang of anxiety and a beating heart. However you wake up, morning rituals can help to set the tone for the day. On happier days, these rituals can be a way of making sure the good feelings last and that you carry this sense of ease and calm through the day. During periods of stress, distress and pain, however, when the day doesn't feel like a bright new day, and you wake up with that heavy feeling of being stuck, perhaps even wanting to cry, those very same rituals can help shift your energy, provide a gentle uplift to your mood and press reset on your day. Simple practices soon turn into habits and become second nature, allowing you to get into the right frame of mind first thing in the morning, ready to tackle the day ahead with more oomph and positivity.

Some of these rituals are more specifically Ayurvedic; others induce positive emotions. They all help you feel energized, and physically and emotionally detox. Make a little time, even if it's just a few minutes, to uplift and ground yourself. If you're in a rush, then rush slowly! You will carry the energy of the morning through your day, so try to be mindful about setting the right tone for yourself.

Furthermore, instilling some of these practices into your morning routine will mean they become a part of you, and you'll have them to hand when you need to face those difficult days.

# START THE DAY

**Waking early** ∾ According to Ayurveda, we should sleep when it's dark and wake with the sunrise, so the ideal time to sleep is between 10pm and 6am. These are the hours that are most rejuvenating, when our cells get repaired, our organs get a recharge, our digestive system gets a rest and our short-term memories are consolidated. Our biorhythms are programmed to follow nature's rhythms, which is why sunrise is the natural time for our bodies to awaken.

I've always been a natural night owl and therefore waking early can be a struggle. However, I have changed my pattern and have started waking up around 7 or 7.30am, which for me is definitely early. A decade or so ago, I was working as a travel journalist and writing my novel late into the night, trying to get everything done while the world slept. I was going to sleep at 3 or 4am. However, this often meant nodding off for the last hour or half an hour, making my time highly unproductive.

Once I started waking up early, I realized how much I can get done first thing in the morning, whether it's opening my little notebook and jotting down inspirations and ideas, or doing *pranayama* breathing, as well as a few key stretches, or simply taking a little more time to get out of bed. Those few moments before getting out of bed, a few moments of silence with yourself, taking deep breaths and expressing gratitude, are moments that can inject positivity into the day ahead, a sense of mindfulness that you can carry through the day and an all-pervading calmness.

**Saying thank you** ᶜᵔ I always try to begin the day with a spirited and spritely 'thanks', at some point before I leave home in the morning. Sometimes I list a few things that I'm thankful for, either aloud or in my head or by writing them down – this was something I started doing when I was depressed and lonely, when I went to sleep and awoke with a very heavy feeling each and every day. This little gesture or acknowledgement of the small but significant things in life brings about a spark of energy but also makes gratitude a habit, so that there is a sense of abundance, not a lack, on a daily basis. I might not feel this gratitude all through the day – we all have moments of anger, sadness or self-pity – but it remains under the surface, ready to be summoned when I need it. Over time, marking the beginning of the day with a few words of gratitude has encouraged atoms of happiness to spread further, to enter my grasp.

**Smiling** ᶜᵔ There are happy days, there are normal, routine days and there are days when we wake up and we're filled with sadness or anxiety. By adopting certain practices into our routine, the factors that negatively affect our emotions have a little less impact and our overall wellbeing will improve, one day at a time. Starting the day with a smile, whether it comes naturally or feels forced, even if happiness feels impossible for you right now, will quickly become a habit; it can make you think of a happy memory, possibly even make you laugh, and by releasing the feel-good neurotransmitters, dopamine, endorphins and serotonin, it can relax your body, lift your mood and potentially even lower your heart rate and blood pressure. Even if, lying in bed, the sheer act of smiling makes you feel silly initially, this might just make you laugh. This small and entirely effortless act of smiling to yourself can have a transformative power and change your day.

**Drinking water from a copper jug** ∾ Start the day by drinking warm water ideally from a pure copper cup or jug filled the night before. Copper makes the water ionic, which helps maintain the body's pH (acid-alkaline) balance. It also helps to balance the three *doshas* – *vata*, *pitta* and *kapha*, and stimulates peristalsis. Copper's antioxidant properties help fight off the free radicals that cause ageing and its antibacterial properties strengthen the immune system. Make sure you get a jug made of pure copper. Avoid scrubbing the copper vessel when washing up; instead, use half a lemon to wash and clean it properly.

**Nature calls** ∾ Clearing your digestive system first thing in the morning is ideal and will be helped along by drinking a few glasses of warm water as soon as you wake up (Ayurveda specifies around a pint). Eating late the night before and not digesting your food properly could prevent bowel movement and regulation. In India, while the local toilets where you have to squat are best avoided, mostly because of cleanliness issues, the squatting position is great for bowel stimulation and digestion. So, if you have sluggish digestion and suffer from constipation, you could get a short stool to rest your feet on while going to the toilet, as this will mimic the squat position and put a little pressure on the bowels. It's a tried and tested method that really works! Of course, the yogic squat is also a great position to just sit in for a minute or two – this could also help. Of course, evacuating in the morning is ideal, but it is more important to be evacuating daily, even if later in the day. Constipation can be painful, can slow you down and make you tired. Sitting with your legs folded underneath you (you could practise the breathing exercises (see pages 40–42) while sitting in this position) is another position that can help with movement in the digestive system.

Constipation, gas and flatulence can be caused by various things from too many acidic foods to how fast you eat and whether you're drinking enough water. Just remember, keeping hydrated is of utmost importance and drinking alcohol and caffeine can really dehydrate you.

**Tongue scraping** ᔋ This might sound odd but scraping the tongue daily removes the build-up of toxins on the tongue and cleanses *ama* from your physiology. In Ayurveda, *ama* is the accumulation of toxins either in the body when we fail to digest food or cleanse properly (the opposite of *ojas*, see page 19), or in the mind, in the form of unprocessed emotions. You can get Ayurvedic tongue scrapers in silver, copper or stainless steel; copper is best due to its antibacterial properties. This should be done after brushing the teeth. Hold both ends of the tongue scraper in each hand, stick your tongue out and scrape off the white coating from the surface of your tongue 2–3 times. Rinse out your mouth afterwards.

**Oil pulling** ❧ Take a tablespoon of sesame or coconut oil and swish it around your mouth for 5 minutes to start with, but try to increase this time each day; you can do it for up to 20 minutes. Then spit out the oil and rinse your mouth out with warm water. Oil pulling helps to keep the gums and teeth healthy by drawing out the harmful bacteria produced during the night, it helps eliminate bad breath and purify the tastebuds. We tend to also hold a lot of tension in our jaw, so the movement of facial muscles while swishing the oil can help loosen these muscles and release some of that stress.

Oil pulling can be done before or after brushing teeth – I choose to do it before. If using coconut oil when solid, the oil might feel thick at first, but it will quickly become thinner as it melts in your mouth.

# BREATHWORK

*Pranayama*, the formal practice of controlling the breath, includes the following simple yogic breathing practices. These help to build energy, aid the *agni* (digestive fire), increase oxygen in the blood and balance the body and the *doshas*, helping you to feel calm and energized. With each inhalation, you get a pump of oxygen in your blood and with each exhalation, carbon dioxide and other toxins are expelled. Over time, these exercises can help to unblock *chakras* where energy is not flowing, expel toxins and increase clarity. It isn't always easy to do them every morning but once you embrace them, breathing deeply and deliberately, even if for a mere 5 minutes, will become an integral part of your morning routine and you'll quickly feel the difference.

**Ujjayi** ∾ Also known as oceanic yogic breathing or victory breath, this technique is good for moments of anxiety, to calm a racing heart. In the morning, it is a perspective setter, a vision opener. It involves breathing in and out of the nasal passage very deeply while constricting the muscles in the back of the throat, which creates a wave-like, oceanic sound.

Start off with 10–20 of these deep breaths, and do more if you can. This is one you can use throughout the day, whenever you need to calm yourself, such as before a meeting or a presentation. If practising this first thing in the morning, you could start with *ujjayi* and then do some of the other breathing exercises.

**Kapal bhatti** ∽ This breathing exercise, also known as 'breath of fire' or detoxifying breath, is great for digestion and bloating, for energizing through stimulation of the solar plexus, for working the abdominal muscles and thus pulling in the stomach, and for expelling toxins. Once you understand how to do it, you can do it a hundred to several hundred times in one go.

Try to sit in a kneeling position, in *vajrasana*, as this is the optimal position for digestion. Otherwise, sit cross-legged, if you can. You could also sit on a chair. Sit up straight, close the eyes for extra concentration and take a deep inhale into the stomach (you only take this deep inhale once, at the beginning). Expel the air through the nostrils with extra force, giving small contractions or jerks to the stomach muscles each time you exhale, trying to empty the air in the stomach each time. Focus on these short exhales and the inhale will happen naturally – don't try to inhale. You will feel your stomach contract each time and almost empty each time. Do it as many times as you can for 2–5 minutes.

This is an exercise for the morning or during the day but not at night before you sleep as it is energizing rather than relaxing. You can do it once, twice or three times a day. As with all these practices, start off with a few minutes and then build up to 15 minutes.

**Anulom vilom** ✎ This alternate nostril breathing exercise is brilliant for energizing, detoxifying and balancing the *doshas* and the energy in the body. It stimulates both halves of the brain as each nostril is linked to the opposite half of the brain. It also improves lung capacity, helps relieve stress, promotes blood circulation and helps with any blood pressure issues. It is often used to prepare the body for meditation.

Place your thumb and first finger on your nostrils. Then remove your thumb and breathe in through one nostril as much as you can. Hold in the breath for around 5 seconds, keeping the other nostril closed, then put your thumb back and exhale from the other nostril completely. Now do the same for the other nostril, and repeat, alternately opening and closing each nostril, breathing through one and exhaling through the other. Feel your stomach contract and expand each time and be aware of your energy as you do this. Continue for a few minutes and try to do it for longer each day.

# MORNING YOGA

I feel a sense of balance when I do yoga. During my practice, I feel that delicious loosening of muscles and tightness; next comes a gentle calm (I don't necessarily feel calm after every yoga session but over time and after much repetition it can have that effect); and finally there's a release – a release in every sense but most significantly of emotion. Sometimes in yoga, I find to-do lists pouring out of my mind, and at other times it's a retreat. Essentially, though, it brings me to me.

Yoga is as much a philosophy as it is a science. It goes hand in hand with Ayurveda. It is the union of the mind, body and soul, with the ultimate aim being to identify with a higher consciousness. Yoga brings the body to life, massages the internal organs and simultaneously quietens the mind, leading eventually to a state where the body is forgotten and the mind is entirely present. It is the process of going inward and exploring that quiet space, of finding our inner power and strength, of expanding our consciousness.

Morning yoga is energizing, a *vinyasa* flow practice that gets the blood moving, loosening any stiffness, stimulating the lymphatic system and awakening hunger. It may not be realistic to do yoga first thing in the morning every day, but on certain days, when you do have time, a half hour routine of sun salutations and stretches (see below), followed by *pranayama* breathing (see page 40) can get the day off to a winning start.

***Surya namaskara* (sun salutations)** ❧ Sun salutations are meant for the morning. They awaken the energy of the inner sun to stimulate the circulation and digestion at the start of the day, energizing the body. They also open up the front and back of the body. *Surya namaskar* does, in fact, mean bowing to the sun, so while you're doing these salutations, try to visualize the sun or just feel a sense of gratitude for the sun and for the light, to make the ritual all the more special. Think of it as a moving prayer, a fluid flow.

There are different sequences and you can add and change some of the positions or poses – *asanas* – as you go along, but it's important to inhale and exhale from one *asana* of the sun salutation to the next.

- start in *tadasana*, hands together at the heart centre

- inhale and lift your arms overhead to *urdhva hastasana*

- exhale as you lower the arms and fold your torso into *uttanasana*

- either on your fingertips or with your palms flat on the floor, exhale as you bring your right foot back into a lunge and then step the left foot back to meet it, or jump back, both legs together

- inhale forwards into a plank or into half plank with knees down

- exhale and bend your elbows as you lower yourself into *chaturanga dandasana*, chest towards the floor as you would in a press-up

- inhale as you arch your torso up and straighten your arms into upward dog, neck and head facing up

- exhale back to downward dog

- inhale as you step the right foot forwards into a lunge, then bring the left foot to meet it, or jump both feet together to *uttanasana* on an exhalation, still bent over

- inhale as you lift your torso and reach your arms overhead to *urdhva hastasana*

- exhale as you lower your arms and return to *tadasana*, hands folded at your heart centre

- repeat, leading with the left leg.

Start with five of these sun salutations and increase the number as you progress. You can also start adding to the sequence depending on areas of stiffness in the body. Add a low lunge on both sides for a deeper leg stretch. The warrior poses along with extended side angle pose (*trikonasana*), really help to stretch out the sides of the body. A revolved side angle pose (*parivrtta parsvakonasana*) or an extended side angle pose (*utthita parsvakonasana*) stretch and lengthen those sides even more.

On more leisurely mornings, extend your stretch and yoga routine, play morning ragas or uplifting classical music while doing yoga and feel your body loosen and extend, feel the vibrations and the sounds sink into the body and raise your energy. Once you're comfortable with the sequence, play with it, let it turn into your own fluid dance, a *leela* (a divine and creative play). It's your own *vinyasa* flow – *vinyasa* is a yoga flow, moving from asana to asana with the breath, that's meant to add fire and heat in the body.

There are, of course, plenty of videos for *vinyasa* flow and other yoga sequences online that you can follow, but going to a yoga studio near you and trying different classes and teachers is a great way of discovering yoga and figuring out what you like and what works for you.

### On silence

Walking down the street early in the morning, when people are still asleep, dawn is approaching, crisp cold air caressing my skin, I feel the city breathe, and in the park I watch the mist evaporate from the grass. The sound of the wind, a gentle hum carried through the air, leaves rustling above and a sense that nature, all around, is wide awake. I take a deep inhale, I smile and then I yawn into the vast expanse of air. I wonder, as I watch the sky unravel whispers of light, whether I might be walking through the city while it dreams or is this when it is most awake? A moment of silence like gold dust before the world awakes.

Life is filled with sounds and noise, with music and words, with melody and cacophony. In a world where there is so much loneliness, we find comfort in noise and people. Silence can be awkward, ominous and uncomfortable, both with others and in our own company. But inner strength and resilience comes from a place inside, a place of silence, a place of wisdom.

As much as I enjoy silence, as much as I have travelled alone and love being alone, as much as I like venturing into my own thoughts, I recall moments of my life when silence felt utterly deafening. Silence is what filled the vast space of sky stretching in front of me when I was living on the 90th floor of a building in Dubai. It echoed my absolute loneliness, a complete void of happiness, a deep unfulfilled hunger for love and my crushing desire to feel worthy. Now, many years later, silence feels like a big sigh, a hug of home, a welcome journey inward – what I wake up smiling to and find myself immersed in first thing in the morning.

In his book, *The Power of Silence*, Graham Turner explores the spiritual value of silence in India, a country where beeps and horns fill the air, where the chaiwalla bellows at train stations, where people speak at maximum volume even when they're at home, where bells ring in temples, thousands gather to chant together and there is, if you really listen, a rhythm in the daily racket of life.

Yet both Muslims and Hindus alike revere silence. The Sufis, Muslim mystics, achieve union with God through silent communion and love, a connection through the heart; the second way for Islamic scholars (the *ulema*) is contemplation in silence, a silence that is focused on the mind. The Hindus call the vow of silence *maun vrat*. I have been with my spiritual teacher Morari Bapu when he keeps silence for the whole month of Shravan, a month dedicated to Lord Shiva. Many still come to see him during that time. He does his nine-day recitals of Ram Katha, where he speaks about and expands upon the sacred Ram Charit Manas (Ramayana) scripture, during that month, but he only speaks for the few hours of the Katha. When you keep silent for a long time, he says, all the activity in the mind settles down, but you should not *try* to make that happen. 'If I make an effort,' he says, 'that is interference with silence.' Bapu also says that even though silence is the door through which God can enter, 'silence is silence – it should be pure and uninterrupted, and I have so much respect for its power that, if He comes into it, I feel disturbed.' When he speaks for those few hours of Ram Katha, Bapu says he doesn't know how, but he feels like he's in a state of silence, much like the Sufi saints.

The early hours of the morning, when you have just woken up, is often the best time to find silence, to sink into it and to float in its vastness. Here are some morning meditations, some moments of stillness to help you channel into yourself and find magic in this time of silence. Try, if you can, to do one of these for a few minutes before you look at your phone or messages or social media, so that your mind is still floating in the peace from sleep and you immediately transfer this energy, your own energy, into the silence, rather than energy that is perturbed, muddled or over-excited by something you've seen or read.

# WAKE-UP MEDITATIONS

In ancient India, the *kshatriyas* or warrior tribes practised meditation to gain superpowers. Today, our motive for meditation is to clear the mind and find peace in a world filled with thoughts, stress and noise; to find ourselves beneath the external layers of judgement; to find happiness amidst constant change. We meditate on our thoughts to recalibrate our thinking, to plug into ourselves again to remember our own self.

The idea of meditation is to have no motivation. It is simply to become an observer, with no analysis, no judgement and eventually no thoughts. To meditate is to experience and the experience is yourself. In the morning, start with a few minutes of sitting still and listen to your body. Try not to think about the rest of the day. A few moments of meditation can instill a sense of peace inside you, which you can carry with you throughout the day, whatever you are planning to do.

**Meditation 1 ~ Speckles of inspiration** ❧ Sit upright in bed and visualize yourself and your body as entirely empty, a vessel of nothingness. Imagine that you feel the sunlight above you, even if it is winter or it's dark outside, and take a deep breath, inhaling the energy of the sun. As you take this deep inhale, imagine the energy of ideas and inspiration as little specks of light floating around you, glittering as they catch the sunrays. With your next long inhale, imagine these wonderful particles flow inside you. Take more deep breaths, slowing down the breath as much as you possibly can and feel the particles of light energy move through your being, filling the nothingness. With each inhale, visualize more and more bright specks enter your being and with each long exhale, imagine them flutter into your brain and further inside. Allow them to extend through you and into your fingertips. Then, move your fingers, smile, stretch and yawn, then move your hands around your face with a massage-like motion, and open your eyes.

**Meditation 2 ~ Connecting to earth** ⚬ You can do this short meditation anywhere, but ideally you want to be sitting outdoors, so this meditation is ideal for those spring or summer days. As early as possible, take a blanket and sit outside on the grass. Close your eyes and deeply inhale that crisp fresh air. Feel the air on your bare skin, sigh as the sun seeps through and penetrates into your body, sense the grass on your skin. Notice the sounds around you and listen to the music and melody in those sounds, sounds you're hearing because you're actively listening, and then settle into your body. Feel the support of the ground and feel supported by the ground, and with your next deep inhale, imagine the energy, emotions, thoughts and worries move through your body and into the ground. Take three long, deep breaths, chanting 'let' on the inhale and 'go' on the exhale. Observe your body as you yawn and then take a few more deep breaths, holding each breath for 5–10 seconds to absorb more oxygen. You'll feel more awake after this, but there's also a sense of wonder and discovery in these observations, a reminder of the magic of nature and of mother earth as you check in with the sensations in your skin and body and finally let everything go and be absorbed into the earth. With that, feel a sense of being grounded and with each inhale allow yourself to be filled with this sense of awe, this awakening, and let it remain with you throughout your day.

**Meditation 3 ~ Instilling calm** 〜 If your emotions and thoughts are racing, or you feel anxiety grip your heart the moment you open your eyes, or perhaps your heart is pounding and you're sweating, it is so important to try to calm the mind and body the minute you wake up. It's a feeling that is hard to shrug off, especially if you're in the depths of an emotionally draining time of life, a time that seems never-ending and suffocating. This is when a few moments of calm are even more necessary to reset your headspace and heartspace for the day ahead. Make a playlist of calming sounds, classical, uplifting, something that really speaks to your soul and happiness, not music that speaks to your sorrow. Sit upright in bed or on a cushion or bolster on the floor and listen to your playlist. If your mind drifts, let it; be aware of this and bring it back to the sounds. Take deep breaths as you listen, try and do the *ujjayi* form of breathing (see page 40), inhaling and exhaling through the nasal passages, as this calms anxiety. Feel the fear loosen, feel it moving through your veins towards your hands and feet and visualize it falling away from the extremities. As this happens, shake your hands and your feet if you can. Then lie down for a minute in *savasana*, corpse pose, the restorative *asana* usually practised near the end of a yoga session. Lie down on your back, legs comfortably spread and arms relaxed alongside the body with

### Being alone and becoming you

The brilliant orange sphere melted into the horizon and the colours of the sky slowly, gradually and then swiftly changed from pink and purple hues to a deep, ever deepening blue. I was the only person in the ocean as far as I could see, as the soft waves rippled towards me, and I could hear a great silence save for the rhythm of water and waves. I started singing and then I spoke. I spoke to the water, to the breathtaking sky in front of me, to the bright moon behind me, to God, and I felt tears running down my face. The colours had almost disappeared, the blue intensified and the moon shone brighter, and I stood there, my ankles in the water, crying and speaking. Out came the stuff in my head that I don't usually articulate, the thoughts that I keep inside and don't put into words; not anger or pain, just honest thoughts and feelings.

the palms facing either up or down. And then just let the renewed calmness soak into your being. Take today as today, not as part of a certain time of life. Think of the day ahead only and of small things you know will make you happy, whether it's a gym class, playing with a dog or just having a cup of tea in a certain café. Try to make a conscious effort to do those things during the day,

To be absolutely alone and to listen to the silence is something we don't often do. We're always with people, always connected and available. Being alone can, for a few moments, feel lonely, but it is only then, when all the noises fall away, all the familiarity disappears, that you hear your own self, that you're in tune with you.

Being you completely, being natural and effortless in your own state, in who you are, is called *sahajata*. The Indian religious leader and mystic, Rajneesh, also known as Osho, once said, 'Hum hum hone ke liye paida huve hein': 'We have been born to be ourselves, I have been born to be me, not to be anyone else.' Not allowing external judgements and our own intellect to affect us, and to be entirely natural, to not be rigid but to flow like air and water, that is *sahajata*. To find this space, to find ourselves, it is important to spend some time alone, perhaps travelling alone or meditating, and to be happy and comfortable being with our own selves.

so pick things that are actually possible and manageable. Your situation might not change, but we have the power to change the way we deal with it each day and the way we let it affect us in different moments.

## My Morning Playlist ✍

'Summer Breeze in India' – Buddha Vibes

'Nectar Drop' – DJ Drez

'Rebirth' – Midival Punditz

'Rama Bolo' – Ben Leinbach and Jai Uttal

'Ha-Tha (Sun Meets Moon)' – Chinmaya Dunster

'Tangerine Thurmi' – Prem Joshua

'Gajumaru' – Yaima

'Baba Hanuman' – Krishna Das

'Seven Chakra Gayatri Mantra' – Deva Premal

'Surya Namaskar' – Michael Mandrell and Benjy Wertheimer

'Improvisation on the Theme Music from Pather Panchali'
    – Ravi Shankar

'It's Life' – Niraj Chag

'Nothing Else' – Shammi Pithia

*Making Music* – Zakir Hussain (with Hariprasad Chaurasia,
    John McLaughlin, Jan Garbarek)

'Raghupati' – Go-Ray & Duke

# SLOW MORNINGS

Whether it's a relaxing Sunday or even a weekday when you don't have to rush around, treat yourself to a slow morning every once in a while. This is a morning to wake up and go about your morning at leisure, at an unhurried pace, to clear your head. This is a time to be in a new environment, to do something you love doing, to go for a walk. Some of these small rituals I've put together can be done daily, for example, playing morning ragas while you do the *pranayama* breathing (see page 40), but a slow morning is when you can take a little more time over them.

**Burning *agarbatti* and attar to clear your space** ꙮ Growing up, I always woke to the scent of *agarbatti* (incense) burning. It was usually a combination of sandalwood and rose, but there are many different scents. The quality of the incense stick needs to be good: the purer it is, the better for health. Incense sticks calm us down and get rid of negative energy; they are used in meditation and prayer, especially sandalwood. *Attar*, on the other hand, is a strong concentrated scent distilled from flowers, bark, leaves and wood and then blended in a base of sandalwood essential oil.

Introduced by the Moghuls, *attar* is used in Ayurveda for its healing powers and sensuality, and to enhance relaxation and concentration. Ayurveda also places importance on the effect of smell on the brain and consciousness. While some essential oils will calm the mind, others will enliven or have aphrodisiac qualities, for example.

The burning of palo santo to cleanse a space and lift energy has become very popular recently. Palo Santo, meaning 'wood of the saints', is a holy wood with healing, purifying and medicinal properties originating in South America.

**Listening to morning *ragas*** ᴥ A *raga* is a piece of classical Indian music that expresses a particular mood. Music is often defined as the language of emotions and therefore, since our emotions change from dawn to dusk, so also must the music that we listen to. Thus, the *ragas* are associated with different times of day, an association which is governed by the notes and pitch. Some of the *ragas* are even attuned with the seasons. Morning *ragas* are softer and more melodious, able to calm the nerves and lead the mind to meditative states. Early morning music leaves deep impressions on the mind, which is why, in all cultures, this is considered the ideal time for prayers. There are a few *ragas* suitable for early morning listening. 'Raga Bhairav' is probably the most popular and is also considered to be the oldest fundamental *raga* of Hindustani classical music. This particular *raga* is also used as the concluding piece at concerts. It is grave and devotional in mood, invoking peacefulness. The ones we grew up listening to and that my father still plays every morning, were by two well-known Indian vocalists, Rajan and Sajan Misra. You will find plenty of examples online and on Spotify.

**Finding a space** ❧ I have always loved sitting alone in one of my favourite cafés, having a coffee and porridge or a snack, ideally with a fire if it's winter or outdoors if it's summer, somewhere that has bright energy and is an uplifting space. It's a few hours of spending time with my thoughts.

On a morning when you have some time, head to your favourite café for a few hours alone. Whether you're reading the newspaper or magazine, writing in your journal or just people-watching and admiring the place, spending this time alone at an unhurried pace gives your mind time to wander and relax; it helps spark ideas and creative thoughts. You'll also have time to eat while at ease, to chew each bite, to really enjoy your breakfast or morning coffee or chai.

If you're constantly with people in your daily life, then these few hours could restore some of your own energy so that you can get back to everything you need to do feeling refreshed. Spending time alone purposefully is *ekant* – solitude; it's conducive to boosting your mood, restoring your energy and being at peace in yourself. It is not loneliness. And once you get into the habit of giving yourself this time to just be and do as you wish, you'll start valuing its purpose in your life more and more, and make it a ritual.

## The concept of mindfulness

Mindfulness can be seen as the modern interpretation of, and name for, various teachings and practices that originated in Eastern philosophies and spirituality. For example, Buddha said that enlightenment is the end of suffering. Suffering comes from a person's failure to accept change, and this in turn arises from holding on to the past and fearing the future. Therefore, the end of suffering can come only by being here and now, by being entirely present.

This is mindfulness: eating when you eat and sleeping when you sleep; being at one with what you're doing, with the person you're with, with the music you're listening to. Mindfulness means focusing on the present action and not on other thoughts that distract or attach to either the past or the future. This concept of living in the present and being fully immersed in what is happening right now isn't just at the heart of Buddhism. It could be argued that it is the over-arching spiritual core of all religions, where religions meet.

**Doing some movement** ✍ If I haven't done much yoga during the week, I like to build some time to practise yoga into my routine on a slow weekend morning, either alone at home, or in a class, usually the latter. Sometimes, however, it's spinning instead of yoga. The idea is to do whatever movement or exercise you love but don't often get time for, mixing it up and doing something a little different. If you usually go to the gym, then perhaps you could run outdoors. It will give you a different perspective, not to mention all that fresh air. Stop for a morning coffee or tea somewhere, take deep breaths to really inhale the oxygen. If it's a nice day and you have plenty of time, take a book with you and read in a park or in a café – a refreshing and revitalizing change of pace and scenery.

**Pottering** ❧ While the idea of a slow morning is to do something nice for yourself, you can also put this time to good use. In the right frame of mind, pottering around doing small home chores, such as tidying a cupboard or drawer, can be relaxing and very satisfying. Just try to slow things down a little, listen to some calming tunes or do the chores in between other activities, such as reading. Take your time rather than rushing them, as you might normally do.

# CLEANSING CONCOCTIONS

You've probably heard of the expression 'fire in the belly'. According to Ayurveda, we all have an inner *agni*, or digestive fire, in our belly, a fire that needs to be fed and kept alive. Therefore, what we eat and drink is of the utmost importance. Given this, a good way to start the day is with a glass of warm or hot water. Cold water is thought to douse the digestive fire, whereas warm or hot water does the opposite.

After drinking a glass of hot water first thing in the morning, I usually also make a concoction with hot water to really get my digestive juices going. Lemon and lime are detoxifying and the minerals and nutrients in them are alkaline in nature, helping to reduce acidity in the body. From a naturopathic point of view, lemon or lime also gives you potassium while sea salt, Himalayan salt or any good salt gives you sodium, two essential electrolytes we need. The concoctions I have vary throughout the week (either because I don't have time to add everything or I want to mix things up), and I've given several options here. They are good for igniting *agni*, and can all be sipped later in the day as well.

❧ Ginger is very warming, anti-inflammatory and great for metabolism. You can sip on this throughout the day. While I used to grate fresh ginger and put it in my drinks, I've now started taking ground ginger because it is much more concentrated. Try to get organic ginger.

Into a mug of hot water stir the following:

> ½–1 teaspoon ground ginger
> a pinch of sea salt or Himalayan salt
> a few drops of coconut oil

❧ Into a mug of hot water, stir together a mixture of any of the following ingredients. This works as a flush, to get the digestive juices going, cure any cold symptoms and for extra immunity:

> a pinch of ground turmeric
> a pinch of ground cinnamon
> 1 tablespoon apple cider vinegar (helps lower blood sugar)
> a squeeze of lemon or lime (avoid citrus if you have arthritis)
> 2 teaspoons honey, preferably manuka honey

❧ If you have time to prep, make this tonic in advance ready for the week ahead. It's a concoction I created for my café, Chai by Mira. Blend together:

> juice of 5 limes or lemons
> 2.5cm piece of fresh ginger, grated
> ½ teaspoon roasted cumin seeds

You can also blend some fresh turmeric into this if you have it!

ᴄᴏ Every morning, stir a few tablespoons of this tonic into a mug of hot water, add some honey if you like, and sip away. You can also have this in cold water in the summer months as a refreshing drink any time of day.

**Alkalizing juices** ᴄᴏ Green juices and smoothies have become incredibly popular and while these are a great way to get extra nutrition, a bonus of greens, it's best to avoid very sweet smoothies and juices as well as too many ingredients in one go. Our body is made to eat a whole banana but not drink a whole banana, with added nuts, berries, apple juice or almond milk and anything else, all at once. I absolutely love smoothies and could drink them all day, especially since I have a sweet tooth, but whenever I have one, especially if I gulp it down, I'll end up with a stomach ache, often feeling horribly full, and wanting to go to sleep. They can be too intense a cocktail of ingredients for the stomach to digest.

Similarly, how many apples are required for a glass of apple juice? It's far better to eat a whole apple or two. This way, you'll get extra fibre, which is not only great for the digestive system but has the added benefit of slowing the release of sugar into the blood, rather than there being a sudden rush. This can lead to more sustained energy levels.

It's also worth remembering that juices and smoothies usually contain raw vegetables and fruits rather than cooked, so sip and drink them slowly. Maybe have them mid-morning or lunchtime when your digestive system is stronger, rather than first thing in the morning.

Eating according to the seasons and climate is important. If you're in the warmth of Bali, a juice and raw salad might give you the energy you need, but the same lunch in the middle of winter in London may take much longer to digest and make you feel sluggish, in part because you might be eating it under stress during a busy work day and in part because raw food doesn't digest as well in a cold climate. Understanding what works well for your own body in different circumstances is vital.

Lastly, whether to juice or blend? Smoothies are ideal if you don't have much time, as you just put everything in a blender. Juices require a juicer and take a little longer. There are certain vegetables that might be difficult to blend such as celery, bitter gourd, bottle gourd and gooseberries, and therefore it is better to juice them.

Here are a few guideline recipes, but you can pick and choose and use what you have available as well as what's in season. Furthermore, if you know your *dosha* constitution and therefore which vegetables and fruits suit you, it is best to choose accordingly.

Try to stick to vegetables rather than fruits, especially any citrus juices such as orange juice as they are more acidic and can cause a spike in blood sugar levels. Fruits should be eaten rather than juiced.

I've mentioned the vegetables bottle gourd (*dudhi*) and bitter gourd (*karela*) in the juice options below because the bitter taste (bitter gourd is much more bitter) helps stimulate the *agni* (digestive fire) helps absorb and soak up *ama* (toxins) and helps to regulate blood sugar. From a naturopathic perspective, these vegetables are alkalizing for the body. You might not be able to find them in all supermarkets, but they are certainly much more available now than ever before. Indian gooseberry (*amla*) is rich in vitamin C and antioxidants and is one of the key ingredients in the *chyawanprash* paste or jam recommended by Ayurveda to calm the system, reduce inflammation and induce restfulness (see page 233). It's also great for the hair.

- 1 bitter gourd (*karela*), 2 celery stalks, 1 carrot, small piece of fresh ginger

- 2 carrots, 1 beetroot, small piece of fresh ginger, small piece of fresh turmeric

- ¼ bottle gourd (*dudhi*), ½ cucumber, 2–3 Indian gooseberries (*amla*, seasonal), 2.5cm piece of fresh ginger

I've added ginger to all the juices simply because it's so great for the digestive fire and also helps with winter colds and flus. However, if you don't like ginger or don't have it in your kitchen one day, it's totally fine to leave it out. It's all about editing according to your pantry, tastes and needs.

In the same way, you may not have fresh turmeric, so instead, you could stir in a pinch (¼ teaspoon) of ground turmeric if you have it to hand. It's another great ingredient, especially in winter, because it's high in antioxidants and is anti-inflammatory.

# SIMPLE BREAKFASTS

I went through years of yo-yo dieting, obsessing over how fat or thin I felt. I replaced Indian home-cooked food with sweet snacking and disordered eating. My lack of self-worth was reflected in the way I ate and this in turn affected my mood and life, even my marriage. My lack of control in my personal life was entirely reflected in my food habits and vice versa. I gradually slid from being a happy free spirit to feeling crushed by loneliness and obsessed with food, ruled by thoughts of what to eat and when and how to exercise it off. It is only now that I realize how I got myself into this vicious cycle and made it my normal, for so very long.

I think of breakfast as setting the tone for the day. Since the digestive fire or *agni* is quite low in the morning until around 10am, Ayurveda recommends having something that is easy to digest and lightly cooked. It should be nourishing with warming spices to increase metabolism. What you eat will, of course, vary from season to season. In summer, yoghurt, grapefruit and flaxseeds might suffice, possibly with some ground cinnamon or ginger in hot water, and then perhaps a coffee, whereas colder days might call for a hot porridge with stewed cinnamon apples and ginger chai.

Including spices in the morning, anything from ginger and cinnamon to turmeric and black pepper, helps to fire the *agni* (digestive fire). I used to have cinnamon first thing in the morning, usually with lemon or lime and some apple cider vinegar, but I've recently changed to have organic ground ginger as it is very warming for the body. It's good to mix things up, change with the seasons and see what feels right for you.

Having something light and cooked, not too sweet or too spicy, will help you feel balanced in the morning. And do, of course, adapt your breakfast to your taste buds, be that sweet or savoury, and your level of activity – if you have a busy morning ahead, then banana, nuts and yoghurt might give you the right balance of carbohydrates, proteins and fats; if you need to remain focused, try porridge topped with nuts and flaxseeds for their high omega-3 fatty acid content (omega-3 fatty acids play an important role in brain function and development), and then matcha latte or coffee.

Doing *pranayama* breathing exercises (see page 40) before breakfast will help to fire up the digestion and awaken hunger as well as move toxins out of the body, but wait for at least 15 minutes after *pranayama* to eat breakfast.

## CINNAMON PORRIDGE WITH STEWED FRUITS
### AND WALNUTS

*Serves 2*

Porridge is what I grew up eating for breakfast, almost daily. My mother always made it runny, not so thick, and that's how I've liked it ever since. A runnier porridge contains less oats, so your breakfast is lighter. Porridge is especially good in the winter months as it's warm and hearty.

> *for the porridge*
> 6 tablespoons oats
> 1½ mugs water
> ½ mug cow's milk, nut milk or coconut milk
> ½ teaspoon ground cinnamon
> 1 teaspoon ground flaxseeds

> *for the stewed fruits and walnuts*
> 1 apple and/or ½ banana
> a little coconut oil or butter
> 3–4 walnuts
> a few tablespoons water
> 1cm piece of fresh ginger or ground ginger, optional

Soaking the oats the night before is always a good idea as the longer you soak grains, the easier they are to digest.

Place all the ingredients for the porridge in a saucepan and cook for around 5–10 minutes, stirring frequently, adding more water if required.

While the porridge is cooking, make your choice of stewed fruits. Chop the prepared fruit into small chunks and cook in the coconut oil or butter in a small pan for about 5 minutes. Break the walnuts into the fruit and mix together. Add the water so that the apple softens a little. Grate in the ginger or add the ground ginger, if using, and cook for another minute. Cook for longer if you prefer very soft apple.

Once the porridge is done, pour into your bowl and top with the cooked fruits. Add raisins or a little honey if you want to sweeten your porridge, and maybe a spoonful of almond butter if you want it a little richer.

## Saffron bircher

*Serves 2*

Soaking your oats overnight is great for those days when you don't have time to cook in the morning, or if you have an early gym session and want to take something nutritious and filling with you for after the workout. If you want to make this a lighter breakfast, if it's summertime for instance, then add additional fruits, a handful of berries and some chopped banana, and use less oats. Saffron is a great mood-booster; it has been shown to be good for anxiety and depression, and is considered by many to be a natural antidepressant; it also helps with sleep issues and can help improve bone strength. In many Indian desserts, saffron is used in conjunction with cardamom as it has a very subtle flavour which seems to be enhanced by cardamom. I've added cardamom here, but as with all recipes, it's optional!

> 8 tablespoons oats (around 70g)
> 1 mug nut milk or any milk of choice (around 250ml)
> 1 apple, cored and grated
> a handful of blueberries
> 1 tablespoon raisins
> 2 teaspoons chia seeds or flaxseeds
> 1 tablespoon other seeds or nuts of choice (sunflower seeds, pumpkin seeds, walnuts)

a pinch of saffron strands
¼ teaspoon ground cardamom
1 tablespoon yoghurt of choice, optional
a handful of any berries to decorate, optional

Place everything in a bowl or other container, mix together and soak in fridge overnight, or for as long as possible.

## DAILY GREEN SMOOTHIE

*Serves 2*

This recipe is a good base smoothie; you can change it or add to it in order to mix things up. For example, if you prefer coconut milk or almond milk, use this instead of coconut water, or you can add in some chia seeds or flaxseeds, if you like.

2 handfuls of spinach or kale leaves
a large piece of cucumber (around 10cm)
2–3 pitted dates, depending on size
a handful of almonds (around 7–8, soaked overnight or for
    at least 1 hour)
2 glasses coconut water (around 400ml)
2.5cm piece of fresh ginger
a generous squeeze of lemon or lime juice

*optional additions*

1 tablespoon protein powder of your choice, for extra
    protein, or a flavoured version such as vanilla if you
    want some added sweetness

½ banana if you've just done a workout and are craving
    some energy and sweetness

some mint leaves

1 teaspoon chia seeds, flaxseeds or spirulina

Whizz everything together in a blender until smooth, then serve.

## AVOCADO TADKA ON SWEET POTATO TOASTS

*Serves 2*

½ avocado (use a whole one if it's small), peeled, stoned and
    sliced

*for the sweet potato toasts*
4 long slices of sweet potato, 1cm thick
½ teaspoon coconut or any oil

½ teaspoon cumin seeds
½ teaspoon salt, or to taste
¼ teaspoon pepper

*for the yoghurt tadka sauce*
¼ teaspoon rapeseed oil or any oil
a sprinkle of mustard seeds and/or cumin seeds
2 teaspoons sesame seeds
3 tablespoons yoghurt
½ teaspoon salt

*optional garnishes*
fresh coriander leaves
a few roasted almonds, chopped
tamarind and date chutney

You can also add an egg to this meal, if you like.

For the sweet potato toasts, start by placing the sweet potato slices in a saucepan of boiling water for around 5 minutes so they start to soften. This is so they need less time and less oil at the next stage. Remove the sweet potato from the pan and drain the water. Put the oil into a frying pan, then add the cumin seeds and cook for around a minute until a darker brown. Place the sweet potato slices in the pan and add the salt and pepper. Let them cook for 5–10 minutes on one side until they start to brown, then turn them and cook for the same amount of time on the other side.

Meanwhile, for the yoghurt tadka, heat the oil in a small

pan, add in the mustard and/or cumin seeds, let them cook for a couple of minutes on low to medium heat, then add in the sesame seeds. Let the seeds turn brown (1–2 minutes) and then stir this mix into the yoghurt in a bowl along with the salt.

Place the sweet potato toasts on plates and top with the sliced avocado and yoghurt tadka. Garnish with coriander leaves and/or chopped almonds, if you like. A drizzle of tamarind and date chutney can also give it a hit of sweetness and tanginess.

Note: you can prepare the yoghurt tadka sauce and the sweet potato toasts well in advance. If you want to prepare a whole jar of the tadka spice mix, you can keep this in the fridge for a few weeks and sprinkle on dishes and stir into yoghurt whenever you want.

## RICE CONGEE

### *Serves 2*

This soupy rice mixture is very therapeutic, easy on the digestion, healing and calming. It's a traditional breakfast dish in China, but also has a similar name in South India: *kanji*. There are ample ways to make this and you can have sweet and savoury variations. Essentially, it's a gently flavoured rice porridge, with a broth-like consistency. It's great for women who have just started their period because rice seems to help soak up that pain – an ancient secret I learned only in my twenties. I've made a version that is savoury, lightly spiced with cumin and ginger, served with a dollop of yoghurt and some fresh coriander leaves.

> ½ teaspoon coconut oil or any oil
> ½ teaspoon cumin seeds
> ¼ green chilli, finely chopped, optional
> small piece of fresh ginger, grated
> 50g cooked rice (cooked by boiling in double the amount of water to rice for around 30 minutes)
> ¼–½ teaspoon salt, or to taste
>
> *to serve*
> 1 tablespoon yoghurt
> a handful of chopped fresh coriander leaves

Heat the oil in a pan on a low to medium heat. Add the cumin seeds and fry for 1–2 minutes until a darker brown, then stir in the green chilli and ginger. Add the cooked rice and salt and mix well. Now add around one mug of water so that the texture becomes soupy. Serve with yoghurt and coriander leaves.

## Creating a feast

You can easily turn this into a feasting-style meal for family and friends by making bowls of congee, then having lots of toppings in the middle of the table for everyone to make up their bowl as they wish. Toppings could include: spring onions, fresh coriander leaves, yoghurt stirred with salt and a pinch of red chilli powder, chopped tomatoes, lemon or lime quarters, chopped green chillies, sesame seeds, crackers, garlic oil or any herb oil.

## LIGHT YOGHURT BOWLS OR POTS

*Each bowl serves 1*

A small bowl or pot of yoghurt, fruits and nuts makes for a wonderful light breakfast or snack. If you've had breakfast very early and know you'll be hungry mid-morning, pack one of these and take it with you to work.

*Papaya coconut bowl*
1 bowl chopped papaya
1 teaspoon ground flaxseeds
3–5 walnuts, broken into small pieces
1 tablespoon desiccated coconut or coconut chips
2–3 tablespoons coconut yoghurt

*Cardamom raspberry bowl*
7–8 tablespoons coconut yoghurt or any yoghurt
¼ teaspoon ground cardamom
2 teaspoons honey
a handful of raspberries
a few pistachios

*Cinnamon prune bowl*
3–4 dried prunes
¼ teaspoon ground cinnamon
7–8 tablespoons yoghurt of your choice
1 tablespoon toasted pumpkin seeds, or any nuts and seeds
   of choice, optional

Soak the prunes in a small bowl of water overnight with the cinnamon. Remove the seeds from the prunes if needed. Fill the water up to just above the level of the prunes. By the morning, most of the water will be soaked up. In the morning, top your yoghurt with the prunes and any juice in the bowl for extra sweetness. Sprinkle with pumpkin seeds or other nuts/seeds, if you like.

*Optional additions*
Chia seeds (soaked in cold water for 10 minutes), flaxseeds, goji berries, pea protein powder or any protein powder of choice, bee pollen, spirulina, sun chlorella, maca powder, hemp seeds.

*Creating a feast*
You can turn the yoghurt bowls into a feast for lots of people by having an array of toppings in different-sized bowls in the middle of the table: cinnamon apple compote, chia berry compote, saffron honey, papaya slices with lime, soaked prunes, apricot slivers, toasted walnuts and almonds, coconut chips, nut butter, banana slices, cinnamon granola. Everyone can then help themselves to whichever toppings they like.

## Tofu and bean shakshuka

*Serves 2–3*

This is for those days when you crave something savoury and filling. It's light but flavourful, although it's great with a side of wholegrain or rye toast, too. I quite like it on its own, especially because it contains beans.

½ teaspoon salt
½ teaspoon cracked black pepper
a handful of fresh coriander leaves, chopped

*for the tomato sauce*
2 teaspoons coconut or other oil
½ teaspoon mustard seeds, optional
½ onion, roughly chopped
2.5 cm piece of fresh ginger, grated, finely chopped or sliced, optional
½ red pepper, deseeded and finely chopped
1 tomato, chopped
3 tablespoons passata
1 teaspoon paprika
a small pinch of cayenne pepper, optional
2 tablespoons chickpea/gram flour, optional*

* The chickpea flour makes the mixture set more firmly in the pan.

*for the tofu scramble*

1 block of silken tofu, around 300g (you can also use firm
tofu, simply use a fork or masher to break into crumbly
pieces)

½ teaspoon coconut oil or other oil

1 clove garlic, grated

2.5cm piece of fresh ginger, grated

100g (around ¼ can) pinto beans (you could also use
red kidney beans)

a pinch of ground turmeric

½ teaspoon salt

*For the yoghurt sauce*

2 tablespoons yoghurt, optional

a pinch of salt

a pinch of dried red chilli flakes or paprika

a garnish of coriander, optional

Place the silken tofu for the scramble on a few kitchen towels or
kitchen papaer to remove any excess water. Leave for as long as
possible, anything from 10 minutes up to 2 hours. If using firm
tofu, you don't need to do this, just crumble as finely as possible.

To make the tomato sauce, melt the coconut oil in a medium
to large ovenproof frying pan on a low heat. Add the mustard
seeds, if using, and wait for them to start popping, then add the
onion.

Stir the onion on a low to medium heat and when it becomes lightly brown, add the grated ginger, red pepper, tomato, passata, paprika, cayenne pepper and chickpea/gram flour, if using, and let this cook for a few minutes.

In another pan, make the tofu scramble. Melt the coconut oil, then add the garlic and ginger and stir for a minute on a low heat. Break up the tofu into the pan, leaving a few large chunks, but if it all breaks up, that's fine. Stir in the pinto beans. Add the turmeric and salt and stir everything together, then leave to cook for at least 5 minutes, but for as long as you can (15 minutes if possible) on a medium heat.

Make the yoghurt sauce by mixing the yoghurt with the salt and red chilli flakes or paprika in a bowl.

Place the tomato sauce in a pancake or frying pan, then add the cooked tofu, spreading it out in a layer. Let this cook on a low heat for around 10 minutes, then place under a preheated hot grill for a further 5–10 minutes until it browns a little on top.

Season the shakshuka with the salt and cracked black pepper, sprinkle with the coriander and serve with a few spoonfuls of the spiced yoghurt dolloped over it.

# CONCLUSION

I often find that the mornings when I get up and out a little earlier than I need to, when I take a moment to look around and breathe, take a deep inhale of fresh air, when I feel uplifted by smelling the coffee from cafés along the street, when I listen to my favourite mantra or music as I walk, those are the days when I feel more attuned, as though those extra few moments I have to myself before my day really begins have awakened me to the world, instilled in me an alertness that I carry with me all day.

In the same way, eating a healthy breakfast, a small portion, with calmness and at least an hour or two after waking up, sets a tone of ease with food, one that allows me to treat all my meals that day with gratitude rather than guilt.

Having morning rituals is important to instill a sense of mindfulness for the day ahead. Of course, life is fluid and need not be rigid, so being comfortable with changing your morning routine now and again, for instance waking up late one day because you had a late night, or switching the format of your morning, can be equally important because this lets you live with ease, it exercises your adaptability and makes change also a part of your routine.

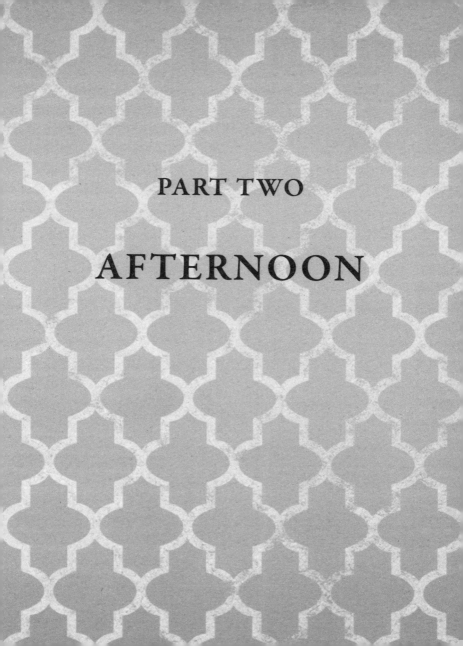

# PART TWO

# AFTERNOON

In between the morning, when we are often at our freshest and most energetic, and the evening, when we usually have a chance to unwind and relax, the afternoon can feel like a long and difficult stretch. By mid-afternoon, we may experience a significant dip in our energy levels and start dozing off, which can be frustrating because it's often when we're required to be at our most alert. This is when we need that fix of coffee and sugar, anything to wake us up and pull us through the rest of the day!

The food we eat for lunch, and whether we chew it well or rush through it and gulp it down, can have an impact on how we feel for the rest of the afternoon – energized or lethargic, productive or bloated, settled or too full. So, I start this section with a whole array of recipe ideas, how to get into the habit of prepping to make it as easy and simple as possible for yourself. Even if you have lots of great food choices and options near your workplace, making your own lunch means that you know exactly what goes into it, and you can ensure it's well balanced. Plus, it will certainly be a cheaper option.

Afternoons can also be a stressful time, when the pressures of our jobs or of looking after children can begin to take their toll on us both physically and mentally. This section recommends a number of rituals for helping you to get through this part of the day; not just to survive the afternoon, but to positively embrace it and get the most out of it.

# LUNCHTIME *AGNI*

**Eating according to *agni*, our digestive fire** ❧ The sun is at its strongest at lunchtime and since our body is attuned to nature, Ayurveda prescribes eating our largest meal at lunchtime. This is when our *agni*, or digestive fire, is at its strongest, so our digestion is strongest. Furthermore, while our body is dominant in two of the three *doshas*, *vata*, *pitta* and *kapha*, these three *doshas* are also dominant at different times of day in each of us. *Pitta*, filled with the energy of fire and transformation, is dominant in the afternoon and therefore able to support our digestion and process the food we eat. However, eating a large meal at lunch can also be counterintuitive if rushed.

**Listening to your lifestyle** ❧ If you're very busy, it's not always possible to have a big meal at lunchtime. Furthermore, if you try to have a large meal at your desk or in between running around and you're stressed, so you don't take the time to chew your food properly, it will be much harder to digest. Having your largest meal at lunchtime could then be counterintuitive. Lastly, after a heavy meal, blood rushes to the stomach and intestines to aid the digestive processes, which deprives the brain of blood, hence we feel sleepy. This is why it is so common to have an afternoon siesta in many countries.

Therefore, while Ayurveda prescribes having the largest meal at lunchtime, if it doesn't work for your lifestyle, which is quite likely in today's world, then try to balance your day by having a smaller meal at lunch, still remembering to chew your food, of course, then have fruit or a simple snack mid-afternoon and a bigger dinner, one that is not too rich or heavy and ideally early in the evening.

To ensure your lunch is balanced and nutritious, something that will give you the energy you need for the rest of the day ahead, I've provided some recipes and meal-planning tips. I've also included options for you to snack on to keep you going throughout the afternoon. The last thing you want is to come home in the evening so ravenous that you end up binge-eating something too rich to digest at night.

**Meals, not snacks** ✏ Eating fuller meals will reduce the urge to snack. I used to be a compulsive snacker, thinking it was better not to eat proper meals and overcompensating with (usually sweet) snacks. My digestion has always been poor but I now realize that snacking really exacerbated this problem. Ayurveda prescribes a 4–6 hour gap between meals without any snacking, to ensure that the *agni* (digestive fire) is strong and ready to digest the next meal. It is important to remember that your food needs time to be digested and you should only eat the next meal once the previous meal has been digested. That said, if you haven't been able to have a filling meal and you get hungry, you might need to snack, and so I've included some good options in this chapter. If your lifestyle is very active, you also might need snacks to give you extra energy. Ayurvedic rules should be treated as guidelines and each person's body and lifestyle is, of course, different.

# EATING RITUALS

When I was growing up, mealtimes were ritualistic and always on time: simple porridge before school and, on most days, a wholesome Gujarati meal as soon as we came home at 5.30pm. This was the *thali*, a traditional Indian meal consisting of all the required food groups and flavours, two or three curries eaten with freshly made rotis, followed by dal, rice and homemade yoghurt. We often ate with our hands and only now do I realize that there is a reason for this, too – with each finger as an extension of the five elements, touching the food stimulates the elements and prepares the *agni* (digestive fire) to bring forth the digestive juices.

We mixed it up, of course; jacket potatoes on Wednesdays, *kichri* (a dish made with rice and mung beans or lentils) usually on Sundays and pizza now and again. Overall, though, there was a routine to our meals and to eating, and a sense of togetherness at mealtimes. It was when I lost that sense of routine when I changed school, and put on weight and developed acne with hormonal changes, that my relationship with food totally changed. Over time, this relationship only worsened, bolstered by my increasing self-esteem issues and influenced by media fads, including the promotion of low-fat diets, having cereal bars instead of meals, and using oil sprays or no oil at all when cooking. I ended up in a vicious cycle of gymming, skipping meals, then bingeing – a cycle that went through good and bad phases, but never really ended.

Constantly thinking about food, about what I was going to eat and what I ate yesterday, feeling fat and trying to feel and look thinner, was a daily battle throughout my university years, my marriage, and even now, though much less frequently. What I finally realized was that I needed to come back to the wonderful nutritious food I had grown up eating, food cooked at home with love. I started to eat proper meals again rather than simply grazing all day, and embraced the ritualistic nature of cooking, the sattvic Ayurvedic nature of Indian home cooking, the basics principles of eating when you're hungry and the absolute need to allow food to digest before having your next meal. Eating well brought about satiation and calmness, took away the guilt and made me realize how simple the answers were, that the solution lay in my own Gujarati home, in the way I had always eaten – only I'd lost my way for a very long time! This was what inspired my food journey and then the publishing of *Saffron Soul*.

When I'm stressed, I tend to revert to snacks and it becomes a slippery slope – it affects my digestion, I start getting those energy slumps again and my mind goes on guilt overdrive. Instilling good habits over time, such as taking a pause before eating, slow breathing and resisting snacking, has really helped me during times of stress. Creating good habits around food will enable you to do these things more naturally and therefore allow you to hopefully gain more calmness before you eat.

**Mindful eating and chewing** ~ In a world where we're always on the go, and eating as we're walking, sitting at our desks or watching TV, we tend to gobble and gulp rather than chew and savour. When we eat without chewing our food properly, the stomach has to work extra hard to turn the food into pulp with stomach acid.

Chewing, and thus mindful eating, is important for the gut, and can help us avoid problems like bloating, indigestion and acidity. Digestion begins in the mouth. Our saliva contains digestive juices and the teeth help to break down large chunks of food, making it easier for the stomach to process what we eat.

You'll also end up eating less if you chew your food well because your brain will receive the signal from your stomach that you're full at the right time rather than when it's too late and you've already eaten too much.

Being mindful when eating is not just about eating consciously but also about mood and energy; it is closely linked to how we feel every day.

Knowing that chewing is so important is one thing, but actually remembering to chew properly is a whole other matter. This is one ritual that deserves to be turned into a habit. To help you do this, try sticking a fun, friendly note on your fridge or on the wall by your dinner table, put reminders on your phone, or use any other method you can think of to remind you to chew.

*Gunas* **or food qualities** ~ I mentioned earlier that there are three *gunas* or qualities in everything, be it in the way we live, in what we eat, and in the energy we have throughout the day. They are: *sattva*, purity and equilibrium, *rajas*, energetic activity, and *tamas*, inertia, and they relate to everything from our levels of consciousness and our personalities to the energy present in the food that we eat.

A tamasic person might be sluggish and selfish, a rajasic person will be full of energy, and the sattvic person will be calm, compassionate and selfless. Similarly, the *gunas* relate to food, defined by how it makes us feel as well as by the qualities it contains.

Sattvic food, such as fruits and anything that is lightly cooked, without spices, of pure quality, is good for the gut and leads to clarity of mind. Rajasic food, which might be more spicy, deep-fried or sugary, stimulates the mind and the body, and might make us feel more aggressive or fired up. And lastly there's tamasic food, including meat, alcohol and things that are processed, which is considered to be sedative, inducing lethargy. It is the interplay of these *gunas* that make up our daily food.

We can apply these ideas to our food choices throughout the day and it is the interplay of these *gunas* in relation to what suits our bodies and digestive systems that determines the dynamics of our way of eating and our way of life. For example, a sattvic breakfast will make us feel calm, ready and energized for the day ahead. Having a piece of cake in the afternoon might be fine for some and therefore be rajasic, but for a person with intolerances, it will be tamasic. One packet of crisps now and again might not damage our system, but it will still be tamasic, as it gives us no nourishment or energy. The food that we eat has an effect on our body, mind and energy levels. Each of us will have one *guna* that is more dominant, and therefore it is good to be aware of and understand the interconnectedness of our food choices, energy state and mind.

*Atithi devo bhava* – **Guest as God** ✺ This mantra, '*atithi devo bhava*', from the Taittiriya Upanishad, literally means 'a guest is equivalent to God'. It is ingrained in Indian families, part of the etiquette of eating, and is demonstrated by serving food with love.

Always eating together when I was growing up and my grandmother's passion for feeding guests and making delicious Gujarati food, inspired me to hold my supper clubs and feasts. Growing up in a large family with my cousins as close to me as my brother and sister, with my aunts and uncles as second parents, and with my grandparents always around, mealtimes always were – and still are – a feast. Conversation revolves around food, what we're eating and who's making what. It is only later in life that I have come to realize how rare and how special this is. Food really is what brings the family together and mealtimes create discussion, interaction, laughter and a general sense of togetherness.

I remember we had lots of dinners – *jamvanas* – for my parents' friends and extended family, where we would have to help, come and say hello and make conversation. The curries would be served up differently when we had guests, always garnished with extra coriander, and there would be an extra curry and a traditional Gujarati side dish like *dhokla, handvo, khandvi* or samosa (there was a time when my mother and aunts would make the samosas from scratch – now we buy them).

The idea of guest is God is felt as soon as you walk into someone's house in India, or any Indian home. There is a feeling of warmth and welcoming, of being fussed over, a sense of celebration. There is even a word for forcing guests to eat: *taan*, something that Indians have done for generations because traditionally guests are shy to take more, so an extra roti and more servings are absolutely necessary. Times have changed now, especially in Indian communities abroad – guests are no longer considered shy and they no longer need or want to be forced to eat – but it is, of course, an ingrained habit and I do now and again still need to pull my plate away when about to be served more! That said, this is all part of the fun, a mealtime of joyful abundance, a feast of colour and delicious dishes.

**Saying grace** ᔆ I went to a school in London where we said grace at the start and end of a meal, a quick half-minute during which we closed our eyes and said thank you to the Lord. Throughout history, people from all cultures and religions have stopped for a few moments to express gratitude for the gift of food. It's a wonderful ritual, a reminder of abundance and nourishment, and acknowledgement of the processes by which the food has ended up on our plate, how the vegetables and ingredients were grown, then cooked and blended to create this soup, the people that have been involved along the way.

Considering again the *agni*, the digestive fire according to Ayurveda, food is an offering to the divine fire in the stomach, it is the means by which we keep that fire alive and burning, and it is this fire that will digest and absorb what the body needs and eliminate the rest. Pausing for a moment before we start eating can also be a reminder to ourselves to eat mindfully and consciously.

**Changing habits** ᴥ Changing the way you eat doesn't just happen overnight – it can, but it requires a huge amount of willpower. It is something that you educate yourself about, train your mind to 'want' to do. Start by eating different foods and changing your tastebuds, something that can take some time, and finally break old habits and make new ones. Everything works together.

If you know you want or need to make a certain change, whether it is drinking less coffee, having less snacks or less sugar, Ayurveda suggests doing it in quarters. If you usually have four coffees a day, have three the next day, then two and then when you can manage it, stick to 1 cup. This makes the process easier and more manageable.

# LUNCH PREP AND RECIPES

Try to take a packed lunch to work so that you know exactly what's in your food, you know that what you're having is balanced and nutritious and you can ensure it's filling enough for you. You can always supplement it with a salad pot or soup from a café near your workplace, in case you like to eat in a café or if you're going for lunch with a friend. You could also plan your weekday lunches by taking a packed lunch say for four days a week and buying lunch on one day.

Do your prep on the evening that you find easiest and make your lunches for the next two or three days. You can prepare the different components and keep them in separate containers in the fridge, then assemble your lunch first thing in the morning or the night before.

**Buddha bowls – a balanced meal** ∾ I love thinking of these daily bowls as Buddha bowls (even though they could very well be served in a box rather than a bowl!). Buddha bowls are so colourful and appealing, and such a joy to arrange and lay eyes on. But the colours are not just for aesthetics. In plant foods, different colours mean different phytonutrients, each with a range of health benefits.

The way Buddha bowls are arranged also makes it easy to see what goes into the bowl, simplifying the concept of healthy eating. Here's an example: sweet potatoes and brown rice are the slow-release carbs, avocado and olive oil are the good fats, spinach or rocket covers the leafy greens, grilled tofu pieces complete the protein, grilled red pepper pieces for colour, flavour and to get some extra veggies in, and lastly a tasty herb dressing, providing even more flavour.

Here is how to prep for the week ahead so you can really vary what you eat each day. Balanced, healthy eating doesn't get any easier!

### Sweet potatoes

This is my favourite and possibly the easiest option for slow-release carbohydrates. but you can also use butternut squash and pumpkin. There are different types of sweet potato but it's the orange ones that contain vitamin A, an essential vitamin needed for growth, immunity, vision and skin.

Take 2–3 sweet potatoes, scrub and scrape off any muddy bits of skin or peel if you prefer, then chop into 1cm cubes. Steam or boil the sweet potato cubes for around 10 minutes until they are lightly cooked but not overcooked. You can now either pan-fry these cubes or roast in the oven. The reason I boil or steam first is because cooking or roasting them then takes less time and requires less oil.

If using a pan: heat ½ teaspoon cumin seeds in 2 teaspoons of coconut oil or any oil, then stir in the sweet potato cubes, add salt (to taste, around ½–1 teaspoon), and cracked black pepper. You can also add ¼ teaspoon ground turmeric, garam masala mix and a touch of ground cinnamon if you have them to hand and you'd like a little more flavour.

If roasting in the oven: preheat the oven to 190°C (375°F/ gas mark 5), toss the cubes in the same amount of oil, spices, salt and pepper and place on a baking tray in the oven to roast for 20–30 minutes until cooked.

Let these cool down before placing in a container in the fridge. They should be good for 4–5 days. It is better to warm them or quickly toss in a pan before eating, simply because warm food is better for digestion, but they can be eaten cold.

## More veggies

Vegetables are a great way to add colour to a meal, to make the meal lighter and add nourishment. They are easy to digest when properly cooked, they combine well with all grains, proteins and fats, and have a wide spectrum of tastes, covering the Ayurvedic spectrum of sweet, bitter, astringent, pungent and salty. Certain vegetables are better suited to certain constitutions – for example, the warming vegetables are best for *vata* and *kapha* types, the cooling ones best for *pitta*; heavy root vegetables are used to balance light *vata* and the leafy greens are prescribed for *kapha*. Overall, however, vegetables are a necessary part of any diet and, lightly spiced, can taste delightful.

When putting the sweet potato into the oven, you could also chop up any other vegetables such as red and yellow peppers, mushrooms, green beans or asparagus, mix them with a little oil, herbs and salt, and place them on another baking tray in the oven.

These can also be eaten raw, but I prefer to cook vegetables where I can, simply because cooked foods are easier to digest. Also, red and yellow peppers, for example, taste sweeter when cooked.

You could also grate carrots or beetroot and add a handful to your bowl.

Lastly, if serving broccoli, I usually boil or steam small broccoli florets, strain the water and keep the florets in a container in the fridge without sautéing or roasting.

### Green leaves

Keep a bag of baby spinach or any leafy greens that you like (rocket, watercress, lettuce) ready to make your bowl or salad.

If using kale, tear or chop into small pieces so you can easily chew the leaves, then massage with a little olive oil, a teaspoon of tahini, and a little salt, paprika and lemon juice. This is my easy way of making kale and tastes delicious when paired with the roasted sweet potato cubes.

### Grains

There's lots of options when it comes to grains, from quinoa and pearl barley to brown rice and black rice. There's also farro, buckwheat and millet.

Rinse the grains a few times under cold running water before cooking, otherwise you retain all the starch.

Cooking times vary from around 20 minutes for quinoa to 50 minutes for brown or black rice. Refrigerate once cooked and cooled.

You could make a few portions of one grain for half the week and another grain for the rest of the week, so you have a variety.

### Good fats

The easiest option is the beautiful, creamy avocado. You only need a few pieces, say a quarter of an avocado, in your meal. If you chop and keep it ready in advance, make sure you squeeze over lots of lemon or lime juice to prevent it from going black.

Olive oil, walnuts and seeds are also a good addition.

### Protein

If you are a vegetarian, there are plenty of protein options: tofu, tempeh, eggs, mung beans, chickpeas, black beans, cottage cheese, quark, etc.

If you're vegan, you can have tofu, tempeh and all the beans.

If you eat meat, there are plenty more protein options.

Tofu prep:

Firm tofu: cut into small pieces and toss in a pan or place in the oven with a little oil, salt, black pepper and a dash of soy sauce or tamari (gluten-free option). You can also add herbs to this, if you like.

Mung beans are a great source of vegetable protein. They can be steamed, boiled or sprouted and added to anything. I also have a recipe for mung bean and sweet potato burger patties in my first book *Saffron Soul*. If you're adding to your lunch bowl, I would suggest rinsing in water and soaking overnight, then boiling for 45 minutes until cooked. Alternatively, if you don't have time to soak them,

then you can just boil for a little longer until the beans
are soft and cooked. You can also cook them in a pressure
cooker.

## Dressings and sauces

Make one or two blended sauces/dressings to use over the week.
These will usually stay fresh in the fridge for 4–5 days.

Coriander and cashew dressing – my go-to dressing:

> 2 handfuls of fresh coriander leaves, a handful of soaked
> cashews, juice of ½ lemon or lime, ½ teaspoon salt or
> to taste, a small green chilli (optional), ¼ glass of water
> (basically enough to make the sauce blend properly), a
> sprinkle of cumin seeds and a squeeze of honey. Blend in a
> high-speed blender, taste and make any adjustments. If you
> want to make it creamier,
> add more cashews or even a few tablespoons of Greek
> yoghurt.

Chilli yoghurt:

> Mix together a few tablespoons of thick yoghurt with a
> pinch of red chilli powder, some paprika, salt and lime juice.
> Add a little brown sugar or honey if you want a touch of
> sweetness.

Roasted red pepper dressing:

> Roast pieces of deseeded red pepper in the oven or sauté
> in a pan (cooking it makes it sweeter). Soak a handful of
> cashews in water preferably overnight but for at least an
> hour, then blend together with the roasted red pepper, a
> dash of water, salt, lemon or lime, a small garlic clove and
> some optional dried red chilli flakes. Taste and make any
> adjustments.

Balsamic tahini:

> This is super simple, literally stirring together tahini with
> balsamic vinegar, salt and a little water. The water just helps
> to bring everything together into a dressing.

Homemade vegan chipotle:

> Stir together 1 tablespoon tahini, 5 tablespoons yoghurt,
> 2 tablespoons balsamic vinegar, 2 teaspoons paprika, ¼
> teaspoon salt, ½ teaspoon mustard, 1 teaspoon tomato
> purée and the juice of around ½ lime or lemon.

Ready-made options:

> If time is tight, you can use hummus, but add a little lime,
> paprika and olive oil to it to make it into a liquid dressing.
>
> If you like pesto, you could also add a couple of teaspoons
> of pesto to your hummus pot and stir it together to make a

hummus pesto dressing. Add a handful of freshly chopped herbs such as parsley or coriander, to bring some freshness and flavour.

### Extras

— Cherry tomatoes, halved, for colour, texture, flavour

— Handful of edamame beans, steamed, for extra protein

— Handful of sweetcorn – if I have time, I like to grill a corn on the cob and slice off the kernels, but you can always add canned sweetcorn for flavour and variation

— Soaked sunflower seeds: soak overnight in a bowl of cold water, strain the water, and sprinkle on your bowl

— Lemon or lime wedge – adds flavour but also covers the sour taste, one of the six tastes each meal should cover according to Ayurveda (see page 20)

— Pack a slice of toast with your salad or some cracker breads if you need something a little more filling.

## KALE AND SWEET POTATO PATTIES

*Makes around 10 medium patties*

I love making patties because they are fairly simple to make and incredibly easy to eat, they go with any dressing or sauce, they add a lot more flavour and substance to a salad, and they can also be eaten with any green or any salad on a piece of toast. Here's my go-to recipe, which you can use as a starting point to experiment with.

2 tablespoons coconut oil or any oil, for cooking

*for the patty mix*
1 small sweet potato (about 150g)
1–2 onions, chopped
2 cloves garlic, grated
1 green chilli, finely chopped, optional
¼ teaspoon ground turmeric
a handful of kale or spinach (around 60g), chopped
1 x 240g can black beans, or any beans, drained and rinsed
½ teaspoon salt
½ teaspoon paprika
½ teaspoon garam masala
½ teaspoon cracked black pepper
2 tablespoons cornflour (*or you can use rice flour or chickpea/gram flour*)

Start by either grating the sweet potato, or roughly chopping it into chunks and then boiling or steaming until soft (about 15 minutes. Both work well, so use whichever is easiest for you! Put all the patty ingredients, including the sweet potato, into a bowl and mix together well, mashing the beans and the sweet potato if you boiled or steamed it. Once everything is mixed well, taste for salt and flavour and adjust if needed. Now divide the mixture into 10 and roll into balls, then slightly flatten the patties between the palms of your hands. These could be any size you want, but I like them medium, around 5cm in diameter.

Put a large frying pan on a medium heat and when hot, place the patties in the pan, adding a few drops of oil around each one. Let each patty cook on one side and then turn over and cook on the other side. Keep turning until browned and cooked through, around 5–8 minutes in total.

These patties are a great addition to any Buddha bowl. Try 2–3 patties with a side of brown rice, chopped avocado, boiled broccoli, roasted red peppers, spiced yoghurt and coriander and cashew dressing. But you can serve the patties with anything you like, or even have by themselves on a piece of brown toast or in a bun with some salad.

## Salads

Salads can be light or filling, raw or cooked. I love simple leafy greens in the summer, but winter calls for something hearty like sweet potato wedges. Here are a few easy ideas that work well for any season, each with a variety of textures.

**Easy kale with avo dressing** 〜 Kale with cooked quinoa or barley, and soaked sunflower seeds, with a dressing made with mashed avocado, tahini, salt, lime juice and olive oil. Garnish with plenty of cranberries.

**Masala sweet potato** 〜 Sweet potato wedges or cubes (around 300g for 2 people), boiled for 10 minutes and then cooked in a pan or roasted in the oven with ½ teaspoon garam masala, ¼ teaspoon ground cinnamon, salt to taste and a drizzle of oil (any type). Once cooked, serve with roasted almonds and chilli yoghurt or any of the dressings above. You could even add to the kale salad above. Garnish with thin slivers of red chilli, fresh coriander leaves and black sesame seeds.

**Herb quinoa** ∾ Boil around 50g quinoa until cooked, then drain and mix with a handful of fresh coriander or parsley or both, a handful of goji berries (soaked in water for 10 minutes), some lightly toasted flaked almond, salt and black pepper. Make a dressing of lemon juice, balsamic vinegar, tahini and water and mix with the salad. Garnish with more coriander and more almond flakes.

### Eating out

If you don't want to make a packed lunch every day and have places to choose from near your workplace, go for healthy, satisfying options, such as:

— In the summer, a fresh and filling salad with some crackers on the side or a packet of baked crisps if you need something salty with your salad. Raw foods such as salads are a little harder to digest and so chewing each mouthful properly is even more important. If you know what you like from a café but you find that it doesn't always fill you, then take a pot of grilled tofu, cooked sweet potato or some extra avocado, for example, to add to it. This will make the meal more satisfying and stop you from buying an extra pot of something after the meal.

— In the winter, a hearty soup with wholegrain toast is always a great idea for all that warmth and nourishment.

If you prefer a sandwich, try to choose one with some greens in the filling and remember to chew well. Everything is good in balance and if you're not allergic to wheat or gluten, there's no reason not to have bread, but it's important to chew it well.

— Ramen bowls have recently gained popularity, and are another great option, especially in the colder months. It is harder to really chew noodles, but do try to chew as much as you can.

# WELLBEING AT WORK

Whether you are working in an office or at home, it's important to adopt some healthy work practices for the sake of both your wellbeing and your productivity. Work can also be a source of stress and anxiety and I provide a number of rituals in this section that can help you to cope with these.

**Sitting up** ❧ Carrying a heavy bag, sitting at a desk all day, hunching over the keyboard . . . these seemingly innocuous things can put a strain on your neck and back and over time can trigger back issues. Eventually, poor posture can result in the back becoming more and more curved. Remind yourself to sit upright. Set a reminder on your phone every two hours to check in with your posture or put a bright, motivating note by the side of your desk saying 'Sit up'. Pull your stomach in and use your abdominal muscles to hold your torso upright. Humans weren't made to sit at a desk all day, so this is a modern-day problem and the only way to correct it is by correcting the way we sit. Posture should be automatic and the more we remind ourselves to sit up and not bend over, the more naturally we will do it.

**Practising better posture** ❧ Poor posture not only affects the spine but also impacts the digestive process by compressing the gut, giving it less space to do its work. Our posture determines how easily blood can flow around the body, and the digestive process requires blood flowing to the gut. Bad posture can obstruct this blood flow, making digestion more sluggish, which can lead to gas and bloating.

**Keeping your computer at eye-level** ❧ Keeping your computer or laptop at eye level is the easiest way to ensure you don't bend over or hunch when you work. This simple thing will keep your neck straight and prevent you from developing back issues from curvature and neck strain. If you're working at home or in a café, you could place a few books or a tray under the laptop to raise your laptop to eye level.

**Stretching at your desk** ❧

- Roll your shoulders back a few times a day, especially if they tend to get tight.

- Move your head from side to side and slowly rotate your neck in each direction a couple of times a day.

- Rotate your wrists a few times a day. If you can, turn your fingers so they are pointing backwards and then press your palms against the top of your desk. This will really stretch your wrists.

- For a quick back stretch, interlock your fingers, face your palms outwards and stretch your arms up and back. Go as far as you can so that your back fully lengthens and stretches. You can either do this standing up or if you're sitting, then use the chair for support.

❧ You can also rotate both ways against your chair by turning to your left and right and holding the chair on each side to give your back a side stretch.

**Stretching your lower back and hips** ❧ If you can find somewhere to do this, try to sit in a squat position for a few seconds, especially if you get tight in your hips. Move your balance from one side to the other and sink into where it feels tight. This can also help with digestion and stomach cramps.

If you feel self-conscious about any of this, do a quick few seconds in the loo!

**Taking a lunchtime class** ❧ If you find it hard to get up early to do a class and you want to feel re-energized for the afternoon, an exercise class or yoga class during your lunchbreak might be the perfect thing. You could find out if there is a gym or yoga studio near you. A quick workout at lunchtime breaks up the day and may just give you that necessary shot of energy. Endorphins, 'feel-good' hormones, are released from the brain during exercise, which is why we feel that high afterwards. Exercising also increases oxygen and blood flow to the brain, which can boost productivity. In the winter, it will also warm you up! You could start by attending a class once or twice a week and see how you feel. You can, of course, do your own workout at the gym, or even at home or in the park, but the shared effort of group exercise can be very motivating.

**Making time for a walk** ⮑ Try to go for a brisk walk at lunchtime – it's a great way to refresh your mind, reboot your day, boost your circulation and increase the oxygen supply to all your cells, including your brain, giving you a burst of energy and focus. If you take a packed lunch or buy your lunch in a café, you could walk to a park to eat it if there's one nearby, or you could walk before or after you eat. Even a quick few minutes of being in nature can relax and destress the body and the mind. Natural sunlight also stimulates the brain and can up your vitamin D levels.

**Getting out into nature** ⮑ Spending time in nature, walking on the earth, breathing fresh air, inhaling the scent and sight of the majestic trees, noticing the movement of branches and the sunlight play through the leaves, hearing their rustling, becoming immersed in that wonderful smell of the earth, the lingering sweet, damp aroma after it has rained, as though the rain has literally extracted the scent from the ground and left it hanging in the air. It is entirely rejuvenating and refreshing. There are lots of words to describe that feeling, the instinctive sense of relief when we're surrounded by blossoming trees, the internal sigh, the instant freedom and vastness of mind. Perhaps this feeling is akin to qualia, the individual consciousness and qualities of an

## Tree worship, walks in nature and forest bathing

Meandering through the streets of Mumbai, I often come across trees and stop and observe for a minute to marvel at their incredible trunks, a mass of shaded tubes that wind around each other like serpents as they travel from the ground up to the branches of the tree, so intricate and beautiful and ancient that they transport me to another era. There's something majestic and sacred about trees. And then, like Shiva's dreadlocks and matted hair, a multitude of tangled ropes hang from the branches and float in mid air, making their journey back to the ground. I imagine these trees of life, blissfully living century to century, seeing gods and kings and Buddhas and other people come and go, filled with vibrations of meditations and thoughts, fulfilling wishes and storing energies. Each one a universe of stories and history.

Tree worship is a part of life in India. In fact, the earliest temple was the tree, with the deity enshrined beneath; and each Buddha was associated with his own tree called *bodhi vriksha* (*vriksha* meaning tree) or *chaitya vriksha*, under which he attained enlightenment. Rudra, one form of Shiva, is also linked with the rudraksha tree (*Elaeocarpus ganitrus*) and therefore, those who worship Shiva often wear a *mala* (rosary) made with seeds of the rudraksha tree. Then there's the beautiful tulsi plant, the holy basil, which traditionally occupies the central position in the courtyard of the house. Tulsi has medicinal properties and the leaves are used even now in Ayurvedic tea concoctions and medicines. Many also wear *malas* made from the roots or stems of the tulsi tree, associated with Lord Vishnu or Krishna.

The sacredness of trees is not bound by religion – many Sufi saints (of Islamic faith) lived beneath trees and when they died, they would be buried there. This place would then become a shrine, a *dargah*. Even now, if you visit a *dargah* such as Haji Ali in Mumbai, you can tie a red-and-yellow string on the branches of the tree outside the mausoleum or to the window trellis. In Punjab, Guru Nanak received enlightenment under the Indian Plum tree and he described the tree as a saviour of creation.

At Indian ceremonies, Indians break a coconut shell at the beginning of a new chapter in life, such as moving into a new home. When the wedding car leaves with the bride and the groom after the wedding ceremony, they often drive over a coconut shell. This is done to ensure the blessings of the gods.

experience. The Japanese have a word for that feeling of mystery and awe, that feeling too deep for words: *yugen*. I wonder if the Sanskrit word *shunyata* is similar to this, experiencing the vastness of nothingness and the clarity that lies therein, or the concept of *mushin* in Zen Buddhism, meaning mindlessness, which is being free of the mind and thoughts and entirely present.

Both Shinto and Buddhism, Japan's official religions, believe in the power of the forest as the realm of the divine. The Japanese also have a word for this experience of walking in the forest, hearing the birds sing, feeling the wind brush the skin, smelling the flowers, observing the leaves, the change in colour – it is called forest-bathing or *shinrin-yoku*. This is simply being in nature, connecting through our senses, observing and absorbing everything around us, revelling in its beauty, and thus 'bathing' in it. Being immersed in nature, opening our senses and being in harmony with the natural world can help us heal and make us happy. According to Ayurveda, we have come from this earth, we are not born into it, and therefore being in nature brings us home and connects us with our own true selves.

*Shinrin-yoku* has been shown to lower the concentration of cortisol, the stress hormone, as well as lower our pulse rate and blood pressure. Even if you live in a city, you can get similar benefits by walking through a nearby park or an area of woodland. You could explore different parks or choose an alternative walk to work that involves some form of nature, just to give you that sense of upliftment each day.

# AFTERNOON ENERGY

## Tackling sleepiness

There are some days when, no matter how much sleep you have had, you'll just feel a slump in the afternoon. Perhaps even be falling asleep at your desk. There are various reasons why this could be happening and if it's happening to you it's worth understanding them, especially if it's happening regularly, so you can tackle it. On those days when you feel this tired, ask yourself the following questions:

**Am I drinking enough water?** ∿ Dehydration can cause tiredness; in fact, it is one of the main causes of tiredness. Your alertness and mood are all affected if you're not drinking enough water. An easy way to see if you're having enough water is by checking the colour of your urine: pale yellow means you're hydrating well whereas dark yellow probably means you need more water. Keep a large bottle by your desk and keep refilling it. Add a squeeze of lemon if you want to enhance the flavour and aid digestion. If you're keeping a bottle there but forgetting to drink the water, stick a 'Drink Me' label on it, or buy a brightly coloured bottle, so it attracts your attention. Or even set a reminder on your phone.

Sometimes, it's the simplest things that will get you into the habit. Once you get used to drinking more water, you'll realize how much you need it and so you will naturally start reaching for it.

**Will coffee really wake me up?** ❧ One of those quick-fix answers, a well-deserved break, an excuse to get fresh air, coffee is often the first thing we think of to tackle that mid-afternoon slump. However, caffeine is very dehydrating and therefore, if a lack of water is the cause of your tiredness, you'll be dehydrating yourself even more by drinking coffee. Your body also becomes used to the caffeine fix very quickly, so you might feel you need more coffee over time to give you that same effect. Furthermore, if it's late in the afternoon, your nighttime sleep might get affected, as it takes 3–5 hours for your body to eliminate half of the caffeine and longer to eliminate the rest. Even if you're the kind of person that sleeps very well, it could disrupt the amount of deep sleep you get or make you a little restless during the night, preventing you from getting the optimum level of sleep you need. If you think you need coffee, but you know you might be having too much, then have one or two cups less each day and replace it with something else. Here are a few options:

- ❧ **Matcha** – this green powder made from ground green tea leaves has been used by monks for centuries to keep alert during meditation. Matcha has a similar amount of caffeine to a cup of brewed coffee, and only slightly less than an espresso, but the buzz is more energizing and longer-lasting.

It also calms the mind, is brimming with antioxidants and tastes delicious with either water or milk. You could stir matcha into hot water, add a dash of ground cinnamon and then add a little cold milk (any milk) over the top. Many cafés now make matcha lattes.

- **Cacao** – cacao in hot water is my preferred drink on days when I'm craving chocolate but don't want to eat sugar. Cocoa or raw cacao is so rich and full of flavour. Just stir a teaspoon into hot water. You could, of course, stir this into hot milk, rather like having a very pure hot chocolate. If you need a touch of sweetness, add some honey or maple syrup. I often add peppermint essential oil to this – it's great for the belly!

- **Turmeric** – a little turmeric in milk or even hot water is another great way of satisfying a craving for something warming and soothing. Turmeric has a whole range of benefits, but at this time of day it can improve the mind's ability to focus, since it increases the levels of growth hormone in the brain.

- **Tummy tip:** if you get stomach pains or cramps, buy a bottle of peppermint essential oil and add one or two drops to your preferred drink.

**Have I eaten too much for lunch?** ✑ Have you eaten more than usual or had something different today? The stomach might still be in the process of digesting your meal, and with all the blood rushing to the colon, there's not enough blood flowing to the brain, hence the sleepiness. If this is the case, consider reducing the quantity of your lunch or changing what you're eating and see what feels better. Remember to always chew well. If tiredness persists, you could start keeping a diary of exactly what you're eating every day and making a note of how you feel during the day. This would be very useful if you were then to see a nutritionist, naturopath, Chinese doctor or Ayurvedic practitioner, so that you can figure out the root cause of the issue.

**Checking for deficiencies** 〜 If tiredness is constant, get a blood test and check for iron levels, vitamin D, vitamin B12 and magnesium. A deficiency in any of these can result in tiredness. Ideally, we want to get all our vitamins and minerals from our food, but it can be difficult to get and to absorb the levels that we need.

- **Vegetarians and vegans** are more likely to be low in iron and therefore more likely to be anemic compared to meat eaters. This is because red meats are very high in iron. Greens, dark leafy greens and eggs are also good sources of iron. The main symptoms of iron deficiency are exhaustion and sleepiness. If you're taking supplements, be aware that iron tablets can cause constipation; liquid iron is easier on the stomach.

- **Vitamin D** is absorbed through the skin. Darker skin has more of the pigment melanin, which can reduce the absorption of vitamin D. Therefore, while there are foods containing vitamin D, such as fish and milk, it might not be enough for those with darker skin – especially if they're living in areas where the sun is weaker. A vitamin D supplement will certainly help in this case.

- **Magnesium deficiency** can cause insomnia and restless sleep, and can heighten stress levels; stress also depletes the body of magnesium. We can get magnesium from dark leafy greens, milk, seeds and nuts, meats and unprocessed whole grains, but we may not be eating enough, or our body may not be absorbing the nutrients properly. A supplement can make a difference to your sleep and stress levels.

- Since the main source of **vitamin B12** is meat and dairy, vegetarians and vegans are more likely to be deficient in B12. This vitamin is needed to produce healthy red blood cells and so a deficiency can cause anemia. It also becomes harder for the body to absorb B12 as you get older. Vitamin B12 injections are the most effective, but you can also take a supplement.

**Going for a walk** ⮌ A quick walk will get your heart rate up, improve blood circulation and give you more energy. The access to sunlight will also make you feel more awake. Take some long, deep breaths or practice *ujjayi* breathing as you walk (see page 40), which will send more oxygen to the brain and energize you.

**Using scents** ❧ Just as a strong smell of coffee might be enough to wake you up in the morning, there are certain scents that are known to have energizing effects. Carrying a couple of essential oils with you, or leaving them by your desk might be just the thing you need when you're falling asleep in the middle of the day. Citrus scents like lemon and grapefruit are great for mental stimulation and help boost the happy hormone serotonin; peppermint has a rejuvenating and awakening effect; while rosemary is a memory booster and makes us more alert.

## If you have a headache

Both stress and dehydration are common triggers of tension-type headaches and migraines. Here's a few simple remedies to help ease your headache:

- start by increasing the amount of water you drink daily in case it is dehydration that is causing the headache

- massage the points where the brows and nose meet

- walk outside to get some fresh air and oxygen

- slow down the breathing and take deep breaths

- ❧ use peppermint essential oil to massage the temples

- ❧ magnesium is known to be very effective in helping reduce headaches

- ❧ sip on fresh ginger tea or stir ground ginger into hot water

- ❧ mix together a little ground ginger with water to form a paste, lie on your back and rub on your forehead and temples, then rest for 15 minutes or as long as you can

I would also suggest looking into craniosacral therapy which is a gentle holistic therapy manipulating the pressure and circulation of cerebrospinal fluid, the fluid that surrounds and cushions the brain and spinal cord. This calms the central nervous system and is very relaxing. Marma therapy (see page 190) would also be very effective if you can find a good marma therapist (see page 245).

## Pick-me-up snacks

Sometimes, when you haven't had a filling lunch or you know you're having to work late and therefore dinner might be later than usual, you may need something small to keep you going, to give you a little more energy and fill that hunger. Here are a few simple snack options that you can take with you to work:

- a mix of nuts, seeds and raisins, prunes or dried apricots

- yoghurt with chia seeds, flaxseeds and nuts and a little honey

- walnuts and a few pieces of dark chocolate

- apple, pear or a small bowl of mixed fruits

- dates with nuts or dates with almond butter or any nut butter

- energy balls: you can make a batch and then take a couple with you to work. Blitz in a high-speed blender or warm the dates in a pan and melt them with the rest of the ingredients, then roll into bitesize balls and store in fridge. Combinations that work well include:

  — dates, nut butter, ground cinnamon or ground ginger

  — oats, dried apricots, cashews, vanilla and coconut

  — dates, any nut butter, cacao, chia seeds

- Avocado on rye or any crackerbreads with salt, black pepper and lemon juice. This is really simple as you can just take the ingredients with you and prepare your snack at work.

- Yoghurt pot with avocado, salt, black pepper, roasted nuts, perhaps with some baked crisps as a side.

Dates and other dried fruits contain fibre, vitamins and minerals.

For example, dates are high in iron and in B vitamins, which are both great for energy. Their fibre content is beneficial for digestion.

The key is balance and knowing your body! Indulging now and again is totally fine, but it is also important to practise restraint and have resolve. Varying your options will make healthy snacking more sustainable.

## Digestive aids

Sometimes in the afternoon, we may feel the effects of a heavy meal from the night before, or we may have eaten a lunch that doesn't sit well with us. It can be difficult to get through the afternoon with this feeling of discomfort and unease. Here are a few infusions that can help with digestion throughout the day. They are both preventative and curative. I suggest keeping a small jar of these by your desk and using them on different days (a small piece of fresh ginger should last you 1–2 weeks if you're using a few thin slices a couple of times a week).

**Mint leaves** 〜 Brew fresh mint leaves in hot water for a few minutes, then cool down the water and drink. You could even brew the leaves in a mug of hot water and then add this concentrated mix of mint leaves and hot water to your large bottle of water (immersing the leaves in hot water first will mean that the mint is more infused and concentrated).

**Ground ginger or ginger juice** 〜 I used to grate fresh ginger and add it to boiling water. Grating the ginger means the juices really seep into the water. If you're chopping the ginger, make sure the pieces are small so that the juices are released. However, I've now started taking ground ginger in hot water as this is a much more concentrated form of ginger. You can do either, though I'd say the powder is much easier. Buy a large pack of organic ground ginger and just keep by your desk and at home. This drink can be sipped through the day to reduce any cramps or discomfort from indigestion, but it has so many other benefits, such as warming the body from the inside, something that I certainly need as I'm always cold! Squeeze in lemon or lime juice for additional flavour and to further aid digestion.

**Fennel or cumin seeds** 〜 Both of these seeds are great for digestion, and stimulating and strengthening the digestive fire. I sometimes boil 1–2 litres of water with a teaspoon of both seeds for a few minutes (although you can boil it for longer), then let it cool down and fill my bottle to drink all day. You can place these seeds in a teabag so they're easier to remove. Or you can leave them in and chew on them later. I love chewing them! Additional options to this tea are coriander seeds and ajwain or carom seeds, both of which also enhance digestion.

**Ground cinnamon** ◡ This is a warming and natural sweet spice that not only adds flavour to any food and drink, but also helps to relieve stomach cramps, reduce flatulence and help digestion. Simply stir ground cinnamon into hot water, with a spoonful of honey if you like (ideally good-quality honey). Cinnamon also helps to lower blood sugar levels and is anti-inflammatory and therefore good for things like muscle soreness or menstrual pain.

**Peppermint essential oil** ◡ Buy a small bottle of peppermint essential oil and add one or two drops of this to whichever drink you like – or even just hot water. I love adding it to cacao powder stirred into hot water and my matcha latte. Peppermint is great for a bloated tummy and irritable bowel syndrome (IBS) and calms stress. IBS is, in fact, often caused by extra stress and therefore easing stress will ease the digestive processes. Peppermint oil is also good for nausea and freshening the breath. But it is very concentrated, so you will only need one drop, perhaps two. You could, of course, have peppermint tea leaves, but the essential oil is much more concentrated and therefore more effective.

# COPING WITH STRESS

When we're stressed, we feel a tightening in the stomach, and we may start sweating and feel our heart pace. This is a neurological and hormonal response to stress. What's going on in the body is a release of adrenaline, as well as the release of glucocorticoids (an example of which is cortisol) from the adrenal glands. Together, these hormones increase the heartbeat and blood pressure, they slow digestion, suppress the immune system and mobilize energy from the liver and fat cells. In the short term, they help us cope with sudden stress, called the fight or flight response. It is when we experience this stress for long periods of time and in excess that stress can cause physical issues and disease. Yes, meditating and practising yoga can greatly help with ongoing stress, but what can we do in those sudden moments when we need to collect our thoughts, calm our minds and make progress with our work and day? How do we settle our nerves and deal with a situation?

**Using the breath** ❧ Elongating and deepening the breath can help us stay grounded and calm us in high-stress environments and moments of anxiety. This relaxed breath helps high blood pressure by dilating the blood vessels and slowing down the heart rate.

So take a few minutes to close your eyes and breathe deeply at a very slow pace, the simplest form of *pranayama*. This will help decrease the blood pressure and relax the body. Visualize the hum of thoughts settle like dust and feel your agitation dissipate. The deep breath increases the supply of oxygen to the brain and stimulates the parasympathetic nervous system, which promotes a state of calmness.

Breathing allows us to figure out our fight or flight response to a situation or a person, to take a deliberate pause, to give us that extra second to think before acting. When our ancestors were faced with a threat, they had a split second before making a decision. Did they run, fight or freeze? Rather like two animals: does the deer run or fight the lion? In our modern world, however, it's unlikely that we would have to face such an immediate life-threatening decision. The threats we face might be different, maybe not as sudden or as urgent, but whether it's making a big life decision or deciding on a deal, or even sitting in traffic on the way to work, this will turn on the stress response. Taking a moment to pause, to breathe, changes the way we might approach a situation and allows us to think more rationally and calmly.

**Returning to the here and now** ⌇ Simultaneously, mindfulness, remembering to be present in all that we do, could prevent the mind from dwelling on the past and worrying about the future, the two things that affect how we are feeling about the present moment – which is often the cause of our stress. Of course, thinking about the past and the future is not something we can easily prevent ourselves from doing. Mindfulness is a practice that we gradually start instilling, whether by a constant effort to let go or a reminder that we stick on our wall so that we see it first thing in the morning and last thing at night. Over time, it will become a habit and we will do it automatically.

### Observing my thought bubbles

I imagine thought bubbles floating around me, bouncing above my head as I walk. One becomes larger, inspires another to form, then drifts as it makes space for yet another that has appeared. It pops before I get a chance to capture the thought, moving somewhere into the abyss, hidden until a time when I rummage through zillions of bubbles to find it again. The odd thought makes a random appearance, maybe pushed forward by the sheer number collecting up there, and falls straight into my hands. I make an effort to take note, send an email to myself, then will it to float away. It's incredible how many thoughts we have, so many that we often don't know even where they came from, a train of bubbles, just like a conversation where you stop for a moment and wonder how you got there. And that's the beauty of it. Not understanding or being able to rewind and unwind. Having faith that where you are now is where you are meant to be; being content with the thoughts and conversations you're having, the place you're in and the life you're living. Not fighting it, allowing yourself to be content in the now yet working for and believing in where you're going, all the while allowing and accepting the bits of unknown to insert themselves in different parts of your life, taking solace in the fact that there is a reason for them and someday you may or may not understand that reason. Just like those bubbles that lead to other thoughts that led to an amazing idea, but at the time when you had the first thought you might have thought nothing of it.

**Repeating affirmations** ❧ An affirmation is a phrase or even just a word that sums up a truth you would like to absorb into your life. With repetition, an affirmation can instill self-belief, help you to acquire a quality you need, or start a process of transformation. Repeating affirmations helps to shift unconscious thought patterns, helps to rewire those patterns and move towards positivity. Our thoughts affect everything we do every single day, they impact how we feel about ourselves and how we see the world around us, and so affirmations can be life-changing.

Even if you find it difficult to believe the affirmation initially, repeating it in a meaningful way when going through a difficult time will slowly and gradually lift you from that space of low self-esteem. Think of these affirmations as your own daily mantras of self-belief and love.

The reason for including affirmations in the afternoon section is that they are a quick and easy way to empower yourself or instill calm or do whatever it is you need at the time. Find the right one for you or create your own unique list of affirmations to chant. You can, of course, use affirmations at any time of day.

Here's a few affirmations you can use, or use these as a starting point and create your own. I've taken some from Paramhansa Yogananda who believed in and emphasized the power of affirmations, the ability to manifest intention through repeating the affirmation. He also gave a clear method: sit with the spine erect, close the eyes and gently focus on the point between the brows, then take a deep breath and exhale it three times. Now repeat the affirmation, start loudly, then softly, softer and softer, until your voice becomes a whisper, then gradually repeat it in your mind, without even moving your tongue or lips, in concentration. Deepen the concentration and enter the super conscious realm to help manifest the affirmation.

I've also taken some affirmations from Louise Hay, who believed that affirmations that are used again and again become beliefs and will always produce results. She spoke about writing down your affirmations 10 or 20 times a day, reading them aloud with enthusiasm, making a song out of your affirmations and singing them with joy.

— *When your self-esteem needs a boost*
I am love
I am worthy of love
I am worthy of respect
I accept myself wholly, just as I am
I am whole and perfect the way I am
I love, honour and respect myself
I am enough
I am full of positive energy
I am confident and powerful and kind

— *When you need to decide on something and feel confused*
All that I seek is already within me. *(Louise Hay)*

— *When you're about to enter a meeting and need to feel invigorated*
I am a joyful breeze entering a room. *(Louise Hay)*

— *When you need to feel calm in the midst of intense difficulty*
Though the winds of difficulty howl around me, I stand forever calm, at the centre of life's storms. *(Paramhansa Yogananda)*

— *When you feel trapped in your head*
I wish to open my heart
I wish to know my desire

**Tapping or EFT (Emotional Freedom Technique)** 〜 One of my closest friends told me to start tapping every single day while I was going through the lowest dip of my life. She sent me You-Tube videos to follow to simplify the process. At that time, I tried anything that came my way, from working with an energy healer, who I happened to meet through a friend in Dubai, to tapping, something I had never heard of before. When you've sunk into the depths of sadness, it's hard to tell what 'works'. How do you even assess whether something is working? However, I did feel a sense of clearing and strengthening with the tapping.

The basic notion is to tap your fingertips on twelve of the body's meridian points, which, much like acupuncture, stimulates the meridians and allows the energy, the *prana* or the *chi* to flow better. Negative emotions can be caused by a disruption in the body's energy system, which in turn can be caused by a distressing memory. With tapping, you're targeting the disruption, not the memory, replacing the disruption with internal calm. When the energy is flowing well, we experience health and wellbeing naturally.

The points to tap are:

— the side of the left hand (where the little finger is located)

— the middle of the forehead, between the eyes

— the right side of the forehead, just above the outside of the right eyebrow

— the top of the cheekbone under the middle of the right eye

— above the lip under the nose

— the chin, directly under the lips

— the collarbone, at the base of the throat

— under the right arm (lift your arm)

— the crown of the head

Close your eyes, take a deep breath and notice what you're feeling. With your right fingertips, tap these points 3–7 times each, saying the affirmations below as you tap each point. Switch to using your left fingertips and repeat.

— Even though I have this stress, I choose to love and accept myself

— I choose to feel good and I choose to love and honour myself

— I choose to love, honour and accept myself

— I choose to feel brilliant

— I choose to let go of fear

— I choose to feel good

— I deserve to feel good

— I deserve to feel great

If you want to change some of the words or use other affirmations, you certainly can. When I started tapping, I could feel words such as *I love, honour and respect myself* shift things internally and empower me.

**Afternoon playlist** 〜 Here's a small energetic playlist for an afternoon pick-me-up – think Buddha lounge, mantra remix, mood-lifting songs incorporating Indian notes and sounds with drums.

'Tumhaari Maya' – Prem Joshua & Chintan

'Jai Sita Ram' – MC Yogi

'Mangalam' – Prem Joshua

'Sublime Sufi' – Sublime Sufi

'Wandering Sadhu' – Desert Dwellers

'Ramana' – Prem Joshua

'Darbari NYC' – Prem Joshua

'Bodhi Mandala' – Desert Dwellers

'Sufis and Gypsies' – Chinmaya Dunster

'Meera' – Prem Joshua

'Punjab' from *Global Spirit* – Karunesh

'Laughter is the Best Medicine' – Cass McCombs

'Allah Waariyan' – Shafqat Amanat Ali

'Water from a Vine Leaf' – William Orbit

**Making time for *seva* – giving your time and skills** 〜 There is a concept in Indian philosophy called *seva*, which means selfless service. This can translate into any form of giving or service – from volunteering for a cause or for a community event, to doing a deed of goodness for someone on the street or for an elderly person. It could be anything! There are so many studies to show the connection between volunteering and happiness. Serving

## Observing life and living with humour: *maya*

A basic notion in Indian philosophy is the concept of our physical existence, the world, the dream of our waking state known as *maya*, which means magic or illusion. The concept of *maya* is expanded upon in the Sanskrit scripture of *Bhagavad Gita* and is rather like the Matrix: the world being the illusion and our consciousness and the so-called dream state as reality. Understanding this changes the way we perceive situations, the way we perceive the world. It does not mean that we live in this world and tell ourselves each day that none of this is real. Rather, it is living with this awareness. This stepping back and observing helps us to let go of things that have already happened and to not fret about what is to come, which inevitably brings us into the 'now'. Being in the present, finding joy in this moment, this is *ananda*, bliss; it is understanding that the troughs are needed for the peaks to exist, much like the changing seasons, and that we should try to find a sense of joy in both.

the community, helping those less privileged, engaging in social change . . . all these things spread empathy and compassion, increase life satisfaction and make people happier, which in turn means they're likely to give more. Acts of altruism break down barriers in society and bring about human connection, they take us out of our heads and out of our lives, even if only for an hour, shifting our perspective, decreasing stress and making us more content.

**Sharing stories with grandparents and the elderly** ❧ We often go through years of meeting our grandparents, whether regularly or not so often, without ever asking them about their life, their history, their stories and how they're feeling, rather than just how their health is. When I'm alone with my grandparents, the conversation sometimes leads to their journey to London, or leaving Uganda or indeed of life in Uganda, and when they speak of these old times and relay stories so detailed it's like they happened yesterday, their eyes light up. Sharing our life with them and asking them about their health is great, but beyond that, taking the time to delve into stories is a way to connect to who they are as people, to make them feel special and interesting. Of course, this goes for any elderly person, and in a world where there is so much loneliness and there are so many elderly people living alone, sometimes just sitting for an hour with someone, being interested and talking could light up their day.

# MINDFULNESS – BE HERE NOW

When we are trying to deal with something, either in our jobs or at home, it is so easy to be distracted and thrown off course, or to have our judgement impaired. Just one small trigger can set off a whole series of irritations. Someone can say something that ruins our whole day. Or we can be distracted by a personal issue that plays on our mind throughout the day.

Mindfulness helps us to live in the here and now, to be present and focused, in a world of distractions and irritations. It helps us to give our full attention to the tasks or the people we are dealing with, and to get our work done.

**Mindfulness technique 1 ~ Breathe in fresh air and exhale stress** ❧ If you're able to go for a brisk walk for five minutes, or longer, it will help clear your head. Breathe in the fresh air and as you do so, visualize bright oxygen molecules entering your blood stream and your brain. With each exhale, feel your distractions and stress being blown out. Make the exhale forceful if that feels better. Shake your head to let go of whatever it is you are holding on to. With your fingers, massage your jaw and the back of your neck, then roll your shoulders backwards and exhale, willing yourself to let go of any frustration, anxiety, stress or irritation.

Now look around and notice all that is natural or simply look up at the sky and absorb the vastness of that space above you. For a mere moment, smile at this, forgetting everything else. Go back to work or the situation you need to face with this slight shift in mind and mood.

**Mindfulness technique 2 ~ Tune into the body** ⌒ Turn off your phone or put it on silent, and sit upright and close your eyes. In your mind's eye, slowly scan your body and be aware of how you feel, in your chest, stomach, arms, hands, legs and feet, and so on. By feeling what's going on in your body, your focus is shifting away from all those buzzing thoughts. Tune in while taking deep breaths. Feel your heartbeat, and be aware of any pain in your shoulders or anywhere else. Wiggle your toes, move your neck, and just settle into your body. Move around in whichever way feels right. Massage your neck if that's what you need. Stretch your arms. Yawn. All these things will release energy in different parts of the body and allow you to be in tune with what's going on, in this moment. They'll make you aware of where the tension is stored and shift your attention away from your mind and your thoughts, even if it's just for a few moments.

**Mindfulness technique 3 ~ Set an intention** ⌒ Setting an intention can help to bring you into the present moment and carry you through a low mood or a difficult task in a much more positive mindset. It gives a sense of purpose and manifestation to what you're doing. Your intention could be something as simple as 'I will stay steady, calm and focused', or 'I will make space for what I need to do'. The intention needs to have a positive, uplifting tone and not contain any negative words. Ultimately, our destiny is shaped by our deepest intentions. The Upanishads declares, 'You are what your deepest desire is. As your desire is, so is your intention. As your intention is, so is your will. As your will is, so is your deed. As your deed is, so is your destiny.'

When setting your intention, say it out loud or even write it down and keep it by your desk so that you can keep reminding yourself. Set the intention, let it go and don't fixate on the outcome or what that outcome would mean and do for you. Have faith in the wisdom of the universe.

## Awareness and who you surround yourself with

When we meet someone who is full of life and happy or simply exuding a contagious calmness, it energizes us, it lifts us, it cultivates the same feeling within us. In the same way, meeting someone who is complaining or being aggressive or anything else that feels negative, we absorb that very energy and leave feeling more flustered and unhappy. Some people make you jump for joy, while others seem to suck joy away, leaving you feeling like you need to sleep or somehow shake it off. Of course, some of us are more energy sensitive than others, but we can sense even a slight shift within us when we meet different people. This is why it's important to be aware of who we are spending time with. That doesn't mean you get rid of friends who are going through a low moment, a breakup or a difficult period; in fact, you need to be that anchor of strength and positivity for them at this time. Rather, it means cultivating awareness of who affects you in a happy way and in an exhausting way, and slowly shift your life, your energy and more of your time to be in the company of friends and people who make you happy, who energize you and lift you. We might not be a reflection of our friends or those who surround us, but our mood and behaviour is often affected by them, and therefore being conscious of this allows us to live with great awareness. In the same way, we develop an awareness of our own energy.

## Sitting with the sadness

Sometimes something happens that jogs an old memory, and with that comes a stream of emotions. Once as I walked down the street with this rush of overwhelming sadness for something that once was, albeit momentarily, I thought to call a friend, my sister, someone. In fact, I did call. Everyone was busy. And I suddenly realised, as I sat on the train, a few tears rolling down my cheeks, that sometimes, all I need to do is sit with it, feel it and let it pass. Talking about it, meeting a friend – that's great. But after all this time, I realised I just need to feel it in my head, in my heart and appreciate that time that once was and take a moment to appreciate what is now.

Riding through life, there are always going to be relationships, deaths, divorces to get over, whatever it may be. Even years later, when life is better and you have a deeper understanding of the situation, there might still be a hiccough, something that not only brings back the memory, but the emotion and pain, too. But it's a part of your story. It's a key ingredient in the narrative of your life. The sadness of what once was and what isn't now at some point shapes into a glowing gratitude of that time, like a snapshot with a sunset filter, slightly hazy and blurred, making it seem like an old dream, a life to wish for. And then you look at it closely and you realize you're in it. That story was, once upon a time, you.

### Who am I?

When we are born, we are a baby with a name and no other labels. There's infinite potential. Over time, labels appear, from being the sister of or the son of to being a teacher or a fashion stylist. The labels are how we identify ourselves, how we introduce ourselves, the box we put ourselves in. This is natural, yet underneath the layers of labels and attachments is our true essential self, the self we were born as, the self that might still be very much alive, but might also be doused and hidden under stories and trauma and busyness. Spending time alone, meditating or simply reflecting allows us to connect inwards, to reach into that space of emptiness, to find that place of strength. This is not emptiness from feeling lost and lonely; rather, it is the significant place of *shunyata*, nothingness, where clarity of the soul and inner stillness exists. *Who am I?* is not a question that needs an exact or well-defined answer; it is a question that sows the seed of wondering and marvelling, a question that puts day-to-day life and conundrums into perspective. It allows us to look beyond the labels and titles and achievements, to identify ourselves as *who* we are rather than *what* we are, and to always act and live from this place of knowledge and strength.

It is worth asking yourself this question, *Who am I?* Repeat it either out loud or in your mind, and go through the various ways you identify yourself, letting the answers unfold and flow. Slowly, time after time, this question will deepen through the layers of different identities, peeling off the external connections by which you identify yourself. It will take you inside yourself. You may not arrive at a final answer but it's a question that lingers and has endless answers. Close your eyes and listen to the sound of the words reverberate in your mind, and listen to the answers as they surface. Observe your own thought processes as you embark on this soul-searching quest. You might even be inspired to write the list of answers to this question and look at how they develop each time.

# CONCLUSION

The afternoons can seem like the longest part of the day. Whether you are surrounded by high energy, confronted by a negative person, have a win at work, feel shattered, whether you're in pain or feel great after completing a task – try to infuse your afternoon with a little more breathfulness. Try creating a pause before you speak, before you think, creating that extra space that gives you a moment to extract yourself from the situation, to observe it and then deal with it rationally rather than emotionally. Theoretically, of course, it makes sense; but in practice, finding your own tools or taking that pause to collect your thoughts can feel like an elusive concept, out of reach. The emotions involved in a particular situation can be so over-consuming that extracting those emotions from the situation can seem almost impossible. Understanding your own self and figuring out what you need in order to apply steadiness can be an exercise and a process of discovery. Making a few adjustments to the way you deal with situations or people will allow you to optimize your productivity and ensure that a small amount of anxiety, for example, doesn't escalate into something bigger. All these things are about developing a greater sense of your own self, living life with more awareness, and understanding others from this point of self-awareness.

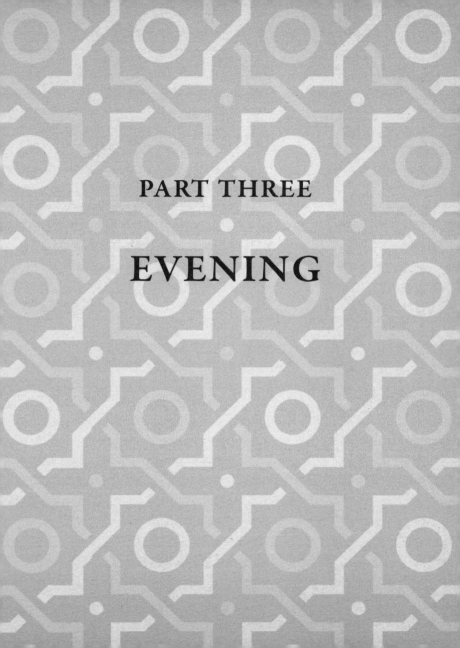

# PART THREE

# EVENING

Arriving home after a busy day, you want to be able to just sigh, let go and relax. But life can be frenetic, filled with social commitments, endless to-do lists, a juggle of passion projects, and parenting. It is difficult to put all this aside and miraculously change moods, to switch to 'home mode'. Life doesn't always allow us to do that. 'Me' time, taking a bath, spending time cooking and eating at the dinner table, making a cup of ginger tea, doing some stretches, chatting to your partner about your day and jotting down the things you're grateful for today – these are best saved for someone who has the luxury of time, or so we often think. But there are only a few precious hours in the evening when you can spend quality time alone or with your loved ones, and therefore leaving stress and job titles and worries behind and moving into husband, wife, sister, friend, me mode is ever so essential. And when we've let things slide, perhaps even let our relationships fall apart, we realize just how important that time can actually be.

This is why you want to create a home that is your sanctuary, a place where you feel relaxed and inspired, where you have personal things, little pieces or elements that tell your story, that keep you engaged, that keep you present, where you can be yourself. Where you can just be.

So, how do you slow down, as quickly as possible? How do you prepare dinner and calm your mind, ready for a good night's sleep? Adequate sleep is not only essential if we are to function properly throughout the day, but is vital for our overall health. It is one of the key pillars of our wellbeing, according to all systems of medicine and healing, including Ayurveda. If I haven't slept well and am feeling tired mid-afternoon, I often find myself eating something sweet to boost my energy levels. However, now that I'm in a better routine with my sleep, I get afternoon slumps less frequently and I am generally much more productive.

# YOUR SPACE TO RELAX

Relaxation is not only about taking time off to do the things we enjoy. It is about quieting our minds and taking a step back, rather than rushing around and feeling the constant need to busy ourselves. Slowing down just a little in between our activities means we stay grounded and stable, it gives us that extra minute to prepare and be ready, to think. For some, meditation will lead to relaxation; for others, meditation might come in the form of playing a guitar; or you might prefer to read something in bed to help you relax or even watch an episode of your favourite TV series. It might be unwise to make watching something in bed every single night into a habit, as this could affect your sleep and might strain your already tired eyes. But if this is what you feel like doing or if it's something that you and your partner do together to unwind, then maybe massage your feet at the same time, or stretch, or even do some deep breathing exercises.

**Your home, your sanctuary** ❧ Your space is your home; it is your sanctuary. You want to wake up and feel happy in your surroundings, feel a spark of energy and be inspired. Decoratively, this might be a bright splash of colour on one wall or it might be a very minimalistic white enhanced by a few plants. Plants freshen the air and add that beautiful energy of nature to your space. Think about the kind of spaces that inject some spirit in you and make you sigh with a wide smile. You want your home to nurture mindfulness, with a sense of space and solace, with freshness and hints of memories, where everything tells a story, but there is also emptiness and room for thoughts to whisper and linger and reveal themselves. All the elements of your space together build your story and become a part of it.

**Cleaning for clarity** ⌒ The clutter and space in your home can really affect your clarity of mind. No matter how big or small your cupboards are, you could be hoarding a lot more than you require. Look through all your things and see what you really need, organize them well and make sure everything has a place. If there are things you don't need regularly (for me that's Indian outfits and holiday kaftans) store them in an organized way in boxes so you know where they are.

**Lighting and mood** ⌒ Lighting, for me, can be the biggest mood setter. It can really make or break it. Going for a dinner party with candles or dim lighting, for example, will be far more atmospheric and will create a relaxed mood, enticing you to stay on, compared to a dinner party with bright lights. Sitting at home curled up on the sofa reading a book calls for candles, perhaps even a fire; doing the very same thing in bright lights could be a little off-putting or at least not as inspiring. Switching to dim lighting in the evening is important in creating your own relaxed space. If the lights happen to be bright in your home, you could get a large lamp that has a dimmer or a couple of different lamps to spread around. Perhaps a large plain candle to evoke that evening mood (though burning scented candles every day might make the air less fresh, even toxic).

**Create your sanctuary** ∽ Monks in Zen temples practise *zazen*, their meditation, beneath a tree or sitting on a rock in their temple garden. Creating your own little garden, even if it is just one or two plants by the window, with a soft blanket and a cushion to sit on, produces a sense of space, somewhere to slow down, take a pause and still the mind.

You can add to this space over time: a *mala* (a garland of beads to use for mantra repetition and focus), your favourite essential oil or balm to massage your temples with, a notebook to jot down your thoughts, a *murthi* statue of Buddha or Ganesha, a special token that you've brought back from holiday, a crystal or rock, perhaps even a lavender eye pillow to place over your eyes when you lie in *savasana* for your calming evening meditation, so that the scent of the lavender soothes you ready for sleep. Then, as you sit and still your mind, this little space of your own can transport

---

### The meaning of a *murti* – statue

If I visit my grandmother at around 9.30am, she is usually in the small *mandir*, the temple room, at home, having lit the small homemade wick in the candle there, her lips moving as she recites her prayers, eyes usually open and engaged with her beautiful *murti*, or deity. She told me how my grandfather carried this *murti* from India to Uganda in 1958 and then she brought it with her to London in 1972 when the Asians were expelled from Uganda. She carried *Ma* – meaning 'mother', short for *Amba Ma* – with her wherever she went.

My spiritual teacher Morari Bapu says that just as a letter from a loved one transforms a mere piece of paper into a treasured keepsake, a *murti* is a way of seeing the Supreme, of finding a path to God. This explains the *pooja,* worship of a statue, in India – the plethora of flower garlands strung around the neck of the statue, and the *prasaad,* the food offerings, that are first offered to the statues of the gods and then to temple visitors.

you to vast green fields, to rivers and mountains, or simply to the silence that is contained within.

There are geometric shapes known as fractals that you only see in nature. There is a lot of science that suggests that when we look at fractals, our cortisol levels (stress levels) go down. Having a plant at home could therefore help us to wind down after a busy day.

# A TIME TO EAT

**When you eat is just as important as what you eat** ∾ The timing of your evening meal is all-important. Trying to sleep on a full stomach is not only uncomfortable but it's not great for digestion, as our digestive fire is not as strong at this time. Undigested food produces *ama* or toxins (see page 38). There are, of course, times when we have to eat late, but it's best to try to avoid this whenever you can.

Ayurveda prescribes eating by around 6pm, which is difficult for me so I tend to eat at about 7.30pm and go to bed around 11pm. This is later than Ayurveda prescribes but it's simply not manageable for me to eat by 6pm. It is important to understand what works for you and your body. Years ago, when I used to stay up writing until 3am, I definitely wasn't doing what was right for my body! But now I've found my happy medium, what I consider to be a balance, and I've worked out how best to achieve that. I do this as often as I can, but there are those days when I'm out a little later or I need to get some urgent work finished. When this happens, I make sure that I stay hydrated and eat properly.

**Cooking with love** ∾ There is energy in everything. When you meet someone and leave feeling vibrant, like you've just had an injection of happiness, this is the effect of that person's positive energy. If you enter a building and something doesn't feel right, you may not be able to put your finger on it, but you want to leave quickly; this is your instinctive sense of negative energy. You may not know the reason, but it could be something to do with the history of the building, something that happened there in the past, or someone who lives there now whose energy is affecting you. We will all be affected by energies in different ways, and we might become aware of them at different times in our lives.

The way we cook, and the thoughts we have while cooking, also infiltrate into our food. Our thoughts are an impulse of energy and this energy is transferred into the food. This is why going to someone's home and being fed by them with love and smiles will satisfy us with a sense of real fulfillment, like we've been given a big hug. It is the company, the laughter, the conversations and the food together that make it such a memorable meal. It is as though the thoughts and love with which food is cooked gives it that extra spark, like a missing ingredient you didn't know was missing until you tried it. Going back to the three *gunas* (see page 92), this also adds a level of sattvic energy to the meal, creating food that lifts your soul and mood. In a similar way that eating while stressed or angry might make it more difficult to digest your meal, food that you cook with love and happy thoughts can be easier to digest and stimulates the production of *ojas* (see page 19), which gives a glow to the skin.

Therefore your state of mind both when you cook and when you eat is an essential part of our ability to absorb the nutrients from our food.

**Cooking your meals as often as you can** 〜 Going out to eat, buying ready meals or ordering takeaways is so simple these days that cooking can seem like too much of a chore. However, it's important to cook our own food, so that we know what goes into it and can ensure that it is healthy with real nutritional value. There is also the pleasure and satisfaction of making something delicious for yourself, or for your loved ones, and then eating it – it's one of the greatest rituals for happiness.

**Applying mindfulness to cooking** 〜 It is entirely invigorating to cook and be present while doing it, to smell the aroma as each ingredient is added, to sense those shifts and changes as the cooking process progresses, to slow down just a little so that you can appreciate each step, to pour focus into the dish, to let that calmness translate into positive energy in the food, and so, to cook with love. Food is energy and our thoughts become this energy and infiltrate into the food we cook, we serve and we eat. Love is the missing ingredient, the key ingredient, that elevates the meal and uplifts our experience.

When I'm magicking up a dish that I have created and I'm so excited to see, smell and taste the result, this is my meditation. Just as, for a dancer, dancing with love is meditation; for a writer, the act of writing with passion and focus is his or her meditation; so it is with cooking for me.

**Eating according to the seasons** ✒ What we eat will depend as much on the season as understanding what suits our body. Our body is in sync with nature, we came from nature, and therefore we should try to eat foods that Mother Nature has created for each season. Foods that are not in season may have travelled from far away, and therefore they might contain preservatives and ripening agents or have wax coatings to make them look fresh. Studies have shown that the longer fresh food is left uneaten, the more nutrients it loses.

Nature provides us with what we need each season. Watermelon, for example, is a summer fruit and provides hydration, whereas winter fruits and vegetables, including dark leafy greens, are high in vitamin C, which is what our body needs in the colder months.

According to Ayurveda, cooked foods are better for us than raw foods, especially in the evening and most especially in the winter. Whereas someone living in a hot climate may find it easy to have a raw diet, a person living through all the seasons will need cooked and hot foods to warm them during the darker winter months.

**Setting the mood** ✒ There's something about lighting candles, dimming the lights, laying the table, setting the scene for dinner, that calms the mood and soothes the soul. It might seem romantic, best saved for special occasions. But the right lighting can transform any dinner – whether with the whole family, a group of friends or you and your partner – into a time to share stories and strengthen togetherness, a way to nourish relationships as well as our bodies. Both of which are key to happiness. Candles can turn a simple dinner into an event.

If you're alone, laying the table or even just putting some music on and lighting a candle sets the mood for enjoying the dinner, for taking time over it if you are able to, or simply being present with the food and remembering to chew and to savour the flavours. This, rather like the Danish concept of hygge, is the art of living with appreciation and care. By really savouring those moments alone, by taking the time to enjoy a cup of chai in your favourite mug, by adorning your home with fresh flowers, you will develop a sense of contentment that will transcend into all aspects of your day and life and impact others.

**Wasting less** ❧ Everything in the natural world occurs in a cycle. There is no concept of waste in nature, because everything occurs in a circle of life. The concept of waste is a fairly new one and therefore it is something that isn't tackled by ancient systems like Ayurveda. We have come to understand, through the impact we are now realizing our waste has on the planet, that there is an urgent need for us all to be conscious and concerned citizens.

It takes anything from five hundred to thousands of years for plastic to break down and decompose. Every piece of plastic made in the last century still exists somewhere today. This not only impacts our planet, our rivers and oceans, and all the creatures in it, there are also plastic particles in the air we breathe, the water we drink and the food we eat. So plastics damage the environment and affect our health.

When we speak about leading a sattvic lifestyle, plastics and other pollutants in our environment are largely out of our control and therefore we can only try to lead as sattvic a life as we possibly can wherever we live. For example, the air will be far purer in the countryside than in the city, but eating well, sleeping well, walking to work, and instilling wellbeing rituals and practices even if we are living in the city will ensure that we are living a happy and sattvic life.

There are also ways to try and minimize our own waste and to spread the message. The idea of zero waste is the desire to live in a world where no resource is wasted, and therefore everything has a purpose and use, rather like in the natural world.

When it comes to food, here are a few ideas:

- Make a very specific weekly list of groceries to ensure there is little to no wastage.

- Use towels and sponges to wipe and clean surfaces rather than overusing paper napkins, kitchen paper and wipes.

- Use up food scraps like carrot skins or vegetables that have lost their colour or that you no longer need by boiling the scraps with water and some cloves of garlic for a couple of hours and making a vegetable stock. Strain the water and keep this water in jars for the week ahead (or you could freeze it). You could use this:

— when making soup instead of vegetable stock cubes or bouillon powder

— to boil your quinoa, rice, risotto or any grain rather than using plain water, giving extra flavour but also additional nutrients

— to boil lentils for dal or soup rather than plain water

— when making creamy pasta sauces instead of milk

❧ Use old newspapers as wrapping paper, painting over one side with a bright colour if you like and then tying with a ribbon.

❧ If you have lots of ginger and turmeric roots left, you could slice into small pieces, place in a jar with lemon juice and salt and use as a pickle with your meals. This is something we have at home daily.

❧ If fruits like apples have become a little soft, therefore not as desirable to eat, then you could peel, core, slice and cook in some coconut oil or ghee and a little water, add some ground cinnamon or any spice you like and eat with porridge.

**Pausing before you eat** &#126; I went to a school where we said a prayer before we ate, thanking the Lord for the gift of food we were about to eat. Only now do I realize the significance and importance of that short pause – a reminder to appreciate the food, a moment to set all things aside to be present with the food, a way to uplift the mind. The prayer or pause can be anything, it can be a simple 'thank you' or a deep breath to bring you to the present moment or a few moments to acknowledge the worries you have, tell them that you will deal with them later and then come to your food with a fresh mind. Eating with fear, worry or anger, or any negative emotion, can affect digestion. Use this pause to also look at the food on your plate, to admire the colours and aromas. By doing this, you bring your conscious awareness to the meal in front of you. This brings into focus the simple joy of eating and it can help assuage the desire to overeat by reminding you to be present and focus on eating and chewing. It is emotions that drive us to overeat and this overeating is more often than not unconscious behaviour. Therefore, by taking a pause before the meal, you're reminding yourself to set any worries and emotions aside and preventing yourself from eating unconsciously.

**Try eating with your fingers** ❧ As a child, I used to observe the expert way in which my grandparents would eat their mix of rice, dal and curd with their fingers, effortlessly making small balls. I ate my roti and curry with my fingers, but when it came to rice, my fingers just felt awkward! I finally improved in my teens and twenties as I travelled around India. But I never really questioned or understood why we ate with our hands.

There are plenty of reasons, I've now realized. Our fingers represent and are extensions of the five elements of nature – earth, water, fire, air and space – and therefore, by eating with our fingers, the food is imbued with the energy of these elements, the energy of the universe. Secondly, our fingers have millions of nerve endings which send signals to the digestive system to start secreting digestive juices, thus leading to better digestion.

This is similar to the nose, where the sensory nerve endings trigger the secretion of saliva and digestive juices, which explains why the aroma of something being cooked can literally make our mouth water and we suddenly find ourselves wanting to eat it. Lastly, touching the food with our fingers allows us to gauge the temperature. We may not realize something is too hot to eat and therefore are more likely to burn our tongues if we don't check. Our fingers naturally give us this information. Eating with our hands is sometimes considered dirty but it's actually hygienic, as long as we wash them.

Certain dishes and cuisines are more conducive to eating with the fingers, or seem more natural to do so, but this understanding of the reasoning behind eating with our hands is something to bear in mind, so that rather than avoid it, you can embrace it, such as when you're having a burrito or when eating an Indian meal.

# DINNER RECIPES

As much as I love experimenting with recipes and finding inspiration from cookbooks, I have my staples, a reliable set of recipes I frequently turn to and that I can edit or add to. These staples do change from time to time, but here's a selection, some guidelines which you can adapt, build on and take ideas from.

**The essential Indian spices** ❧ Every Indian home will have a spice box or *masala dabba,* a circular steel container with separate round compartments for the various spices. Here are some of the essentials:

— cumin seeds

— mustard seeds

— ground turmeric

— ground coriander and ground cumin already mixed

— fenugreek seeds

— red chilli powder

— garam masala – a very useful pre-mixed spice blend you can sprinkle on anything!

Each of these spices has a plethora of health benefits, from aiding digestion to lowering blood cholesterol, and can really be used in any dish, not merely confined to curries. I often add the ground coriander and cumin to my coriander and cashew dressing (see page 103) or stir-fry my tofu with a pinch of cumin seeds.

**Asafoetida** ⮜ Adding a pinch of this strong and rather pungent powder to your cooking will add flavour but also aid digestion and bloating. When eating dishes with lentils and beans, which can naturally create flatulence, spices like cumin seeds, ginger and especially asafoetida help to ease this. Asafoetida can burn easily, so the time to add it is once the *tadka* is done: for example, when the garlic or onion is browned and cooked with mustard seeds and cumin seeds, then add a pinch of asafoetida and quickly stir in whichever vegetable, beans, lentils, etc, you're cooking.

**Ghee** ⮜ Ghee is clarified butter, prescribed by Ayurveda because it increases the *agni* (digestive fire) and is good for all *doshas* or body types. In Ayurvedic cooking, ghee is used to sauté vegetables and for all cooking and baking (not frying). The vegan alternative is coconut oil.

## KICHRI WITH GARLIC, PEAS AND SPINACH
### (also spelt kichdi, kichari)

*Serves 2*

This is the simplest Ayurvedic healing recipe to make at any time of year. It is said to balance the *doshas* and is very calming and purifying for the digestive system. *Kichri* is a simple blend of rice and split mung dal (green) or rice and yellow mung dal (approximately half and half), washed and then mixed and boiled together in a pan for about 45 minutes. It is nourishing and warming, one of those reliable staples my family would have once a week, usually on a Sunday evening. We also had it whenever we came home from holiday or our travels. It's often given to babies and children as well as the elderly and sick – and everyone in between! You can make it entirely plain and eat with a spoonful of ghee or yoghurt, or you can make it with vegetables or serve alongside vegetables or a curry. Here, I've made it with a few simple greens, flavoured with onions and garlic.

I would suggest keeping this mix of split mung dal and rice in the portion of 50/50 ready in a large jar so you don't have to mix it each time. Adding a pinch of asafoetida helps combat any potential bloating issues from the mung beans.

150g kichri mix OR 75g basmati rice and 75g split mung beans

1 tablespoon ghee or coconut oil

½ teaspoon cumin seeds

½ teaspoon mustard seeds

a few fenugreek seeds, optional

1 red onion, sliced

1 or 2 cloves garlic, finely chopped or grated

a pinch of asafoetida

¼ teaspoon ground turmeric

5 tablespoons peas

1 pack of spinach (about 120g)

1½–2 teaspoons salt

750ml water

*to serve (optional):*
fresh coriander leaves
yoghurt

Rinse the kichri mix under cold running water a few times to remove any starch. In a medium pan on a low heat, heat the ghee or coconut oil, then add the cumin seeds, mustard seeds and fenugreek seeds, infusing. When the mustard seeds start to pop, (this will happen after about a minute), add the onion and garlic and cook until they're lightly browned, about 2 minutes, then stir in the asafoetida and turmeric and immediately add the peas and spinach and ½ teaspoon of the salt. Stir this on a medium heat for a few minutes, then add the kichri mix and pour in the water and 1 teaspoon of the remaining salt. Place the lid on the pan and let the kichri cook for 45 minutes on a low to medium heat until all the water is absorbed and the kichri is well cooked.

Once cooked, stir it quickly as though you're whisking, taste and add the remaining salt if required, then garnish with coriander, if you like, and eat with some yoghurt or just by itself. You can also eat with a side of roasted poppadoms.

## MINI SWEET POTATO AND BEETROOT PANCAKES

### *Serves 2*

This is perfect for breakfast or dinner. It's a wonderful way to pack in these colourful root vegetables, plus it's incredibly easy yet so satisfying. You could serve this up for dinner with friends with a chutney or two, some yoghurt, maybe a side of roasted herb broccoli and any other vegetables you like.

1 small (approx. 100g) sweet potato, peeled and grated
50g beetroot, grated
2 tablespoons rice flour
2 tablespoons gram flour
1 tablespoon coconut oil
1 teaspoon cumin seeds
1 red onion, chopped
2 cloves garlic, grated or chopped
4 tablespoons of water
salt, to taste

*optional garnishings*
sliced spring onions
avocado mash or slices
fresh coriander leaves
spiced yoghurt
coriander chutney
balsamic syrup

Start by mixing the grated sweet potato and beetroot into the rice flour and gram flour. Melt half the coconut oil in a medium frying pan on a low heat and add the cumin seeds. Once the cumin seeds have browned slightly, about a minute, add the onion and stir, then add the garlic. Cook for a couple of minutes, until lightly browned. Now add the vegetable batter, stir, then return to mixing bowl and form 4–5 patties/mini pancakes. Place each pancake in frying pan with a teaspoon of oil and fry for around 5–8 minutes, turning regularly until browned on both sides.Remove from pan and allow to cool before serving with whichever garnishings you like. You could also serve with some lightly spiced yoghurt or coriander chutney. Add a drizzle of balsamic syrup, if you like, for extra flavour.

## BOTTLE GOURD AND TOFU CURRY

*Serves 2*

I haven't put many curries in this book, but this is a recent creation, and since bottle gourd is such a great alkalizing vegetable, this is something you could make once a week and eat with rice or quinoa or some roti. If you don't have bottle gourd, you could use courgettes instead.

    1 teaspoon ghee or coconut oil
    ½ teaspoon cumin seeds
    1–2 cloves garlic, finely chopped or grated
    ½ teaspoon ground turmeric
    ½ bottle gourd, peeled, deseeded and chopped into
        2.5cm pieces, around 300g
    200g tofu, chopped into cubes
    ½ teaspoon salt
    1 tomato, chopped

In a medium pan on a low to medium heat, melt the ghee or oil and add the cumin seeds, then add the garlic after about a minute, once the cumin seeds are lightly browned. Stir in the turmeric and then the pieces of bottle gourd and tofu. Add the salt, mix well and let this cook for a few minutes before pouring in half a glass of water. Stir well, then add the tomato just before serving.

## EVERYDAY VEGETABLE STEW

### Serves 2–4

This is a one-pot-wonder dinner where you can use up all those spare vegetables in your fridge. Any leftovers will be perfect for lunch the next day and even the day after that. Serve with a dollop of yoghurt, a few grilled halloumi slices, or an egg – whichever way you like. Of course, you can make it more flavoursome by adding in some chopped or sliced fresh chillies, or extra garlic if you prefer. It's a lovely base recipe which you can experiment with and vary from time to time.

> 200g sweet potato, chopped into cubes or slices
> 2–3 teaspoons coconut oil or any oil
> 1 teaspoon cumin seeds
> 1 red onion, sliced or chopped
> 1–2 cloves garlic, finely chopped
> 1 tomato, chopped or sliced

½ red pepper, deseeded and sliced

½ courgette, sliced into rounds

1½–2 teaspoons salt

80g brown rice, cooked and drained

1 x 400g can black beans or kidney beans

1 teaspoon paprika

½ teaspoon ground coriander

1 tablespoon yoghurt

2–3 tablespoons tamarind and date chutney

a handful of fresh coriander leaves

*To serve (optional)*

yoghurt

tamarind and date chutney

grilled halloumi slices

fried, boiled or poached eggs

Start by boiling the sweet potato for around 10 minutes until a little soft, then strain off the water and set aside. In a large pan on a low to medium heat, melt the oil and add the cumin seeds. After a few minutes, when the cumin is slightly browned, stir in the onion, garlic, tomato, red pepper and courgette and ½ teaspoon of the salt. Mix well and let the vegetables cook for around 10 minutes before adding the cooked brown rice, black or red kidney beans (you can either strain the liquid from the beans or add some of it), paprika, ground coriander, remaining salt, the yoghurt and tamarind and date chutney. Stir well and taste for salt and spices. Garnish with coriander leaves. Serve with an extra dollop of yoghurt, an extra drizzle of tamarind and date chutney, grilled halloumi slices or an egg – whichever you choose.

## YELLOW DAL WITH SPINACH AND EXTRA GINGER

### *Serves 2*

There's nothing quite as comforting as a dal, especially on a cold day. This one is incredibly simple, mellow yet flavourful, with just ginger, turmeric and cumin, and a handful of spinach stirred in right at the end. It's similar to yellow tadka dal that you find at Indian restaurants, but not as intense in flavour. Rather than overpowering it with garlic and chilli, I've used only ginger. You also have the option to add a little coconut milk if you want to make it creamier, but it's also perfect just as it is.

150g moong dal (yellow lentils)
1 teaspoon oil (any type)
1 teaspoon cumin seeds
¼ teaspoon ground turmeric
1-inch piece of fresh ginger, grated
1 litre water
a large handful of spinach leaves
small piece of fresh ginger, thinly sliced

½ teaspoon salt, to taste

2 tablespoons coconut milk, optional

*to serve (optional)*
cooked rice
yoghurt
green coriander and cashew chutney

Rinse the lentils a few times under cold running water to get rid of any extra starch. Heat the oil in a pan on a low to medium heat and cook the cumin seeds for around a minute until a darker brown. Add the turmeric and grated ginger and immediately pour in the water and add the yellow lentils. Boil on a low to medium heat for 30 minutes, stirring regularly, until the lentils are soft and cooked. Add the spinach leaves, thin ginger slices and salt to taste. If using coconut milk, add this at the end when the lentils are cooked and the water is absorbed. Serve with rice and yoghurt and/or green coriander and cashew chutney, if you like.

# COMFORTING DRINKS AND
# SOMETHING SWEET

### HOMEMADE CHAI

Chai is synonymous with India. If you're Indian, it's usually the first thing you drink when you wake up and what you have after your afternoon siesta to give you that burst of life and energy. I have my own chai spice mix, containing seven spices, that I serve at my café, Chai by Mira. Furthermore, different parts of India make chai in very different ways, from boiling it with lots of grated ginger to simply crushing cardamom pods to using a masala spice mix, the way I do. However, the dominant spices are always ginger and cardamom, so you could start off working with those. Here's a few simple ways to make a quick cuppa chai at home.

Boil together the following for 5–10 minutes on a low to medium heat, then strain into a mug and enjoy – the true Indian way:

> 1 mug any milk you like
> 1 English breakfast teabag
> ¼–½ teaspoon ground ginger or 1cm piece of fresh ginger, grated
> ¼ teaspoon ground cardamom (optional)

To make chai directly in your mug:

— place a teabag in your mug as normal

— add ¼ teaspoon of ground ginger, and sugar if you like

— pour over some boiling water from the kettle slowly, stirring as you pour, leaving enough space for milk

— pour in any milk you like (I use almond or oat milk) but again pour slowly and stir as you pour

— serve and enjoy!

## HALDI CHAI, SPICY TURMERIC

Turmeric is going through its hero moment, and for good reason! The golden super spice is radiant with anti-inflammatory and antioxidant powers, great for everything from prevention of colds to healing from an injury or illness. You can get turmeric or golden milk at cafés and restaurants now, but it's really simple to make at home with the addition of a few extra spices to elevate its power. Ginger, for example, amplifies the anti-inflammatory nature of this drink as both these spices help tackle inflammation in the body. Sip on this any time of day at any time of year.

Boil the following together for 10 minutes, then pour into a glass and serve:

> 1 mug any milk you like
> ½ teaspoon ground turmeric
> ¼ teaspoon ground ginger
> ¼ teaspoon ground cinnamon, optional
> a pinch of ground black pepper, optional

## RAAB, SWEET MILLET

*Makes 1 mug or 2 small cups*

Traditionally, this delicious, soothing, creamy hot drink is for breastfeeding mothers to strengthen their muscles and bones after childbirth and to help produce more breastmilk, but it is, in fact, a wonderful winter warmer, especially if you have a cold, with all those healing properties we all need when it's cold and dark outside. Furthermore, since it is for muscles and strength, if you do heavy workouts and weightlifting, this might be just the thing your body needs. It's also great if you're low on energy or have congestion. Millet is rich in fibre, easy to digest, and has a high calcium and iron content, so it's good for vegetarians who can be low in these minerals.

3 teaspoons ghee or coconut oil

½ teaspoon ajwain (carom) seeds

2 tablespoons millet flour

600ml water

2 tablespoons jaggery*

½ teaspoon ground ginger

¼ teaspoon ground turmeric

Melt the ghee or coconut oil in a small pan, add the ajwain seeds and let them darken in colour (about a minute) before stirring in the millet flour. Keep stirring for a few minutes on a low to medium heat until the millet flour is cooked (4–5 minutes). Heat the water in a separate small pan and stir in the jaggery so that it dissolves in the water. Stir the ground ginger and turmeric into the millet mixture, then pour in the water and jaggery. Be very careful as you pour because it will spit. Keep stirring vigorously until the mixture thickens and becomes a soup-like texture. You can make the consistency thinner by adding water if you prefer.

## Optional additions

You could stir in some coconut milk, if you like. You could also make this into a porridge by adding a couple of tablespoons of oats after adding the water and jaggery mixture.

---

\* Jaggery *gur* is a natural Indian sugar, in the form of small, brown rock-like pieces. Can also use coconut sugar or honey.

## Juice pulp oat muffins

*Makes 10 small muffins*

My grandparents have fresh juice every morning, usually a mix of carrot, ginger, apple and beetroot. I was having juice with them one morning and, while clearing up, decided to use the juice pulp rather than throwing it away. I made a small batch of oat muffins using only a few spoonfuls of the juice pulp and they tasted delicious! I topped them with some vegan almond cream cheese and started selling them at my café. They've now become a regular, a great way to use up juice pulp, meaning zero waste, and the pulp adds lots of fibre, making them great for digestion, too.

100g oats
50g raw cashews
50g coconut sugar, jaggery or soft brown sugar
300ml water with 1 tablespoon chia seeds soaked for 10 mins
¼ teaspoon bicarbonate of soda
¼ teaspoon baking powder
5 tablespoons leftover juice pulp
1 teaspoon ground allspice or ground cinnamon
a little soft brown sugar, ground cinnamon and flaked
    almonds for sprinkling, optional

*optional toppings*
almond cream cheese mixed with a little honey
a sprinkle of dried rose petals

Preheat the oven to 190°C (375°F/gas mark 5), then mix together all the ingredients except the brown sugar, cinnamon and flaked almonds for sprinkling, if using, and blend in a high-speed blender. Add a little more water if required (you want a cake-batter consistency). Pour a large spoonful of the batter into each of 10 cups of a cupcake mould or 5 of a muffin mould, filling each around three-quarters full, sprinkle a little brown sugar, cinnamon and almond flakes over the top, if you like, and bake in the oven for around 35–40 minutes. Check that they are baked by piercing all the way through with a fork. If the fork comes out clean, this means the muffins are ready. Allow them to cool in moulds. Will keep for 4–5 days in fridge.

Top each muffin with almond cream cheese and a sprinkle of dried rose petals just before serving, if you like.

# MASSAGE AND ALTERNATIVE THERAPIES

I have a number of younger cousins, and the image of my grandmother massaging them when they were babies is so vivid in my mind. This is, in fact, in accordance with Ayurveda, and so a daily massage for the first few years of a child's life is an ingrained habit in many Indian families. Baby massage might therefore seem like a recent discovery for some of us, but it is, in fact, a very useful rediscovery. If, for example, there is a slight bump on the head or the nose seems a little flattened from childbirth, Indian mothers and grandmothers very slowly and gently, day by day, over weeks, mould them back into shape with oil massage. Touching, stimulating, massaging and nourishing the skin is important throughout life; for an infant, it has been shown that regular caressing can lead to stronger immunity. Of course, when it comes to baby massage, you need to be extra careful and very gentle.

Massage is not just an indulgence, or 'pampering' as we sometimes think of it, but a form of therapy, one that relieves aches and pains, combats fatigue and activates the body's innate healing power. Many civilizations have a long tradition of massage. The first written massage therapies originated in India around 1500 BCE, although it is thought the practice may date back to around 3000 BCE or earlier. The art of 'healing touch' is an important part of Ayurveda, as with all ancient healing systems, and it supplements any healing programme alongside food and yoga.

Massages are good for blood circulation, counteracting muscle tightness, especially in the winter months, and for de-stressing. The build-up of lactic acid in our muscles can cause cramps, fatigue and knots, and since massage directs more blood into the muscles and thus more oxygen, it removes lactic acid by converting it into carbon dioxide and water. Massage oils also nourish the skin.

Massage therapy might seem expensive, but instead of going to a hotel spa, you could find a Thai or Chinese masseur in your local area and try a few different therapists before finding your favourite. Understanding what your body needs will also come with time. I've always needed extra pressure whereas others can't take too much.

Ayurvedic massages, however, are very different to deep tissue or Thai massages. I would suggest doing Ayurvedic massages as part of a wholesome healing package rather than as a one-off. Having been to many Ayurvedic resorts in India and seen how they perform massage, I have come to realize that the oils used, the repetitive firm strokes rather than the ironing out of knots, and the combination of different techniques throughout the day are therapeutic and healing in conjunction with everything else: the daily food and juices, the timing of meals, and, of course, being in a relaxed environment. The main purpose of most Ayurvedic massages is to get those medicated oils properly absorbed into the body and then to rest in the sunshine or sleep and let the oils seep inside and do their work.

One Ayurvedic treatment might relax you, but it won't bring about change and it might not even give you that same sense of freeness that say a Thai or a Swedish deep tissue massage might. It's very important to do regular Ayurvedic massages as part of a whole package, alongside healing cooked foods like *kichri*.

The best therapists will be able to work on realignment and not just massaging into the knots – what I would call intuitive bodywork. Each therapist will have a different approach and you have to find what's right for you. Once in a while, if you can, find someone who can do real bodywork, realigning the body and working on the root cause of any pain or discomfort. I love a deep tissue massage with a therapist who has a lot of strength and who can help to rebalance and realign my body. Go with your instinct and see what works. Massage is the perfect complement to yoga, movement, rest and good diet. Therapies can be expensive, but I would suggest thinking of them as an investment in your own health and longevity. By instilling practices such as not crossing your legs when you're sitting and carrying a backpack rather than a handbag on one shoulder can help you maintain a sense of balance and equilibrium so that the body doesn't go out of alignment so easily.

**Try self-massage** ꙮ Whether we've been sitting at a desk all day, carrying a heavy bag or driving, our necks and backs can get constricted and hold stress and tension. You might feel it in your upper back, your shoulders, your neck or just one side of your lower back. Yoga, Pilates, remembering to correct your posture and daily stretching can all help a great deal, but you could also incorporate daily massage into your routine, even if it is just 5 minutes here and there.

Start by moving the neck gently from side to side, and then in circular motions, then use your fingers to massage the back of your neck, maybe as you move your neck around. Do what feels right and listen to your body. Next, roll the shoulders backwards and if you can, clasp your hands behind your back and stretch them backwards, ideally while standing, but you can also do this while sitting. Then, using your fingers and thumb, massage both sides of your lower back, pelvis and hip area, wherever your body feels tight.

Foam body rollers can be really helpful for self-massage. You can use them all over the body, especially any tight areas, such as the thighs, which you may not be able to massage yourself.

**Give yourself a face massage** ✒ We hold a lot of tension in our jaws because we often clench them when anxious or scared or stressed; sometimes a misalignment in our bodies can start in the jaw. Gently massaging the jaw can release some of this tension. It may not be practical to do this every day, so I suggest two or three times a week. I use a gentle Ayurvedic face oil, but coconut, almond or any other oil is also suitable. Use just a small amount and wipe your face with a hot towel afterwards. Place your fingers on your forehead and use your thumbs to massage your jaw gently, starting at the top of your jaw by your ears, then moving downwards towards the chin. You could also use your knuckles to do this, going back and forth from ear to chin, massaging the entire jaw.

Then gently massage around your eyes, then pinch the brows between your index finger and thumb and move across from the inner to the outer edges, squeezing each part of the brow. Apply as much pressure as feels right in each area. Make this a daily evening habit while you stretch your back, roll the shoulders and rotate the neck, so that you're always relaxing the face along with your stretch routine before you sleep. Be very gentle if you have acne, as massage can be painful. But you might want to avoid face massage altogether because touching the face can spread bacteria.

In Ayurveda, there are certain marma points in the face which correspond to different parts of the body and their functions (see below). While the points in the feet and hands are much more effective to help rectify problems and ease certain issues in the body (reflexology), getting into the habit of massaging points on the face can be a relaxing and rejuvenating practice for daily life. Here's a few:

— *Hanu*, in the middle of the chin, to improve circulation to the face and connect with inner feelings.

— *Gandu*, halfway up the nose on either side, to clear the sinuses and brighten the eyes.

— *Apanga*, in the outer corner of each eye; press away from the eye to relieve eye strain.

— *Ashru Madhya*, below the inner edges of the eyebrows in the inner corner of the eye socket. Gently press away from the eye towards the top of the head to ease eye strain and headaches.

— *Mantha*, on the side of the neck, four finger widths below the earlobes, for circulation and to stimulate the lymph.

— *Karnamula*, behind the ear lobe, where the ear meets the jaw, good for ear congestion, jaw tension and anxiety.

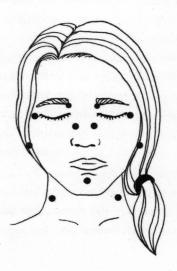

For a detailed explanation on how to massage your own body and face and which points are most effective, read *Absolute Beauty* by Pratima Raichur.

**Reflexology** ❧ Reflexology is a specialist massage on the feet using specific thumb, finger and hand techniques and pressures. It can also be done on the hands and the face, but it's most commonly used on the feet. Our feet are micro-systems of the body, as are our hands and face. By applying pressure to different points, you can have an effect on the corresponding part of the body. Areas of sensitivity usually indicate areas of weakness or parts of the body where there might be an issue or blockage. I recall that when I started having reflexology treatment, after the first session I had an emotional release, and cried a lot; after a few sessions it helped to regulate my periods, as well as easing my digestion. For one of my close friends, reflexology helped to balance her thyroid. For each person, the effects and results will be entirely different. Even if you don't have a specific issue, it can help relax you, enhance certain functions of the body and identify any underlying issues you might have – as with any alternative therapy.

**Marma therapy** ❧ Marma comes from the Sanskrit word *mru*, to kill. Years ago, warriors had knowledge of these points in order to kill their enemies, but this knowledge was also utilized by physicians for healing the wounded. The focus of marma point massage is to manipulate the *prana* (energy), and on a physical level, to alleviate stiff muscles and boost circulation. There are said to be 107 marma points on the body, with the mind as the 108th. Massage of these points, called marma therapy, removes blockages and opens up the energy channels in the body.

I first did marma therapy in an Ayurvedic resort in Kerala and felt an intense relief throughout the process. The therapy was strong and quite painful, but the good kind of pain. Afterwards I had a feeling of utter lightness, a new sense of freedom and movement. Choose a practitioner carefully – there aren't many proper marma practitioners around and you really need someone who knows what they're doing. See my Resources section on page 245.

**Intuitive bodywork** ❧ When you find a brilliant bodywork therapist, what they are able to do through realigning the body can be life-changing. Of course, if you do have some discomfort, it's likely to be not just about alignment – to get the best result, you need to use different modalities such as heat therapy, Chinese herbs and marma therapy, to find a root cause. And, as with Ayurveda or reflexology and acupuncture, this has to be done in conjunction with a lifestyle change, with educating yourself and doing the homework. The therapist that I go to uses Chinese Medicine as her foundation but works on the body intuitively and intelligently while educating, talking through the causes of inflammation and why it's important for the body to try and get rid of this inflammation (often caused by over-consumption of sugar and the body's response to that).

**Acupuncture** ~~> This therapy is rooted in the ancient Chinese system of medicine and involves penetrating the skin with a thin needle at certain points on your body. These points are similar to the *nadis* and *nadichakras* in Ayurveda, through which the *prana* (energy) flows. There are more than 2,000 acupuncture points in the body in Chinese Medicine, all of which are connected by bioenergetic pathways known as meridians through which the *chi* flows. This *chi* is like *prana*, the vital energy which flows through the body; blockages in the *nadis* or meridians that prevent the *prana* or *chi* from flowing freely can lead to imbalances and disease.

Through acupuncture, by working on and unblocking certain channels, the *chi* is able to flow more easily and fluidly. So acupuncture is meant to activate the *chi* and steers it into certain areas where the energy is stuck. This initiates change in the body at a very deep level. Acupuncture is used for anxiety, stress, pain management and fertility, among many other issues, but it is worth noting that even if you don't have any particular issue, complementary therapies like acupuncture can bring about greater balance in the body and mind. Traditionally, acupuncture uses needles and heat, however today, most acupuncturists don't use heat. Of course, if you're having acupuncture, it's necessary to do your homework and to use it as part of a holistic approach. Have your ground ginger in hot water daily to energize yourself from within.

**Others** ～ There are many other treatments, from shiatsu (Japanese) and cupping (Chinese) to gua sha (Chinese) and craniosacral therapy (an offshoot of osteopathy), as well as energy healing such as pranic healing and reiki. It's worth doing a little research and starting somewhere, perhaps experimenting, then finding what works for you. Go with a recommendation and trust your instinct.

# EVENING YOGA

Yin yoga, or restorative yoga (which is more supported, often using props), consisting mainly of long-held, passive floor poses that are designed to calm the mind and stretch the body, is ideal for the evening. After a day of sitting at a desk or in meetings, these stretches will help to ease any tension, loosen tightness and generally relax the body.

These are some of my favourite evening yoga positions for that much-needed deep stretch, each one delicious in how they feel. Every time you do them, increase the number of seconds you hold them so that you get a deep release and really get into the connective tissue. Put soothing music on so that you're inclined to hold the positions rather than rush through them. Holding the poses for longer and 'melting' into them will enhance the benefits they have for your body, mind and soul.

Each of these stretches opens the body up in a different way, hence I've divided them into heart openers, spinal twists and hip openers. While doing these, breathe deeply, a rhythmic breath, visualizing any stress, tightness and worries released with each exhale.

## Heart openers

As we move through life and experience either physical or emotional pain, or both, we try to find ways to protect ourselves. Physically, this translates into rounding the shoulders so that the heart is less vulnerable. This can constrict the *prana*, or energy, flowing to the heart *chakra*, which is called the *anahata*. These postures are great backbends that will open up your shoulders, and they also allow more energy to flow to the heart and thus unblock this vital energy centre.

*Salamba setu bandha sarvangasana* (**supported bridge pose**) ✑
This is my happy place and I can be here for a very long time! This pose releases the back but is also a gentle heart-opener. Lie on the floor with your knees bent and your feet flat on the ground. Lift your hips, so that only your head, arms and feet are on the floor. Add a block either lengthways or upright under your back at the very base of your spine – avoid the lumbar spine. You might need

to go up on your toes to get the block under your back. Then rest in this position for a few minutes or as long as you can.

*Ustrasana* (**camel pose**) ᘛ The mother of all heart-opening poses, the camel pose opens the entire front of the body, challenges core strength and improves spinal, hip and shoulder flexibility. This pose involves a deep backbend, though, so flow through a few sun salutations beforehand (see page 44). Come to a high kneel with your knees hip-distance apart and press your shins and toes into the floor. Place your hands on your lower back with your fingertips pointed downwards. Slowly lean backwards, as far as you can without feeling discomfort. If you are flexible enough, you can hold your heels or ankles. Take three deep breaths here. To come back up, place your hands on your lower back if they're on your heels or ankles, and slowly roll back up. Do this pose three times.

*Bhujangasana* (**cobra pose**) ∾ Start with the sphinx and move into the cobra as the latter is a much deeper back bend. Lie on your stomach, with your elbows underneath your shoulders and your forearms parallel to each other on the floor, like a sphinx. Inhale, and as you exhale, slowly peel your upper body off the floor. Breathe deeply as you remain in this position, shifting up further if you need a deeper stretch. To go into the cobra pose, shift your weight from your forearms to your hands, pushing the floor away gently with your hands.

## Spinal twists

Spiralling the torso around the spine compresses and massages the digestive organs. This stimulates the digestion and metabolism as well as helping the organs flush toxins. The twisting also calms the nervous system and quietens the mind. Hold these poses for a few minutes and take long, deep breaths, moving further into the stretch with each exhale.

***Parivrtta sukhasana* (cross-legged pose with a twist)** ~ Sit upright in a simple cross-legged position and place your right hand on the floor behind you. Bring your left hand to the outside of your right knee and twist to the right, gazing over your right shoulder. Inhale to lengthen your spine and exhale to twist deeper. Hold for a few minutes and then repeat this movement on the other side.

***Supta matsyendrasana* (reclined spinal twist)** ~ This is one of my favourite poses to end a yoga session. Lie on your back, bend your knees and drop both knees to the left. Stretch your arms out

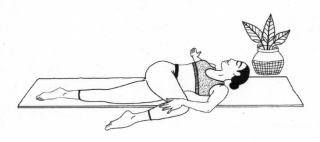

along the floor and gaze over your right shoulder. Straighten your left leg and use your left hand to keep the right knee pressed to the ground to deepen the stretch. You can also place a pillow or a folded blanket under your right knee if it doesn't touch the floor. Hold this for a few minutes or as long as you can, then do the same on the other side.

*Ardha matsyendrasana* (**seated spinal twist**) ～ Sit upright and bend both knees, feet flat on the floor. Thread your right leg under your left, which is still bent, getting your right foot as close to your left buttock as possible. Place your left hand on the floor behind you for support. Now lift your right arm up on a deep inhale, and when you exhale, twist your body to the left and look over your left shoulder. Place your right hand on your left knee, or your right elbow on your left knee for a deeper twist. Hold this for a few minutes or as long as possible and then do exactly the same on the other side.

## Hip openers

We hold a lot of negative emotions in our hips and therefore opening the hips up and deeply stretching them can allow us to release these negative emotions. This can initially be uncomfortable but very soon it will start to feel like a delicious and much-needed kind of discomfort. When I do these poses, it feels as if my body is sighing and letting go.

*Balasana* (**child's pose**) ᔕ A grounding and calming posture, this elongates the spine and releases the hips. Kneel on the floor with your knees hip-width apart, and bring your feet together. Sit back on your heels. Bring your forehead down towards the floor and either stretch out your arms in front of you or lay them down by your side. To deepen the stretch, ask someone to press your back down gently, from top to bottom – such a wonderful feeling.

*Malasana* (**squat pose**) ᔕ This is great for constipation – both physical and emotional! Stand with your feet shoulder-width apart,

inhale and bring your hands together into prayer. Then, keeping your back straight and feet fully on the ground (place them wider apart if necessary), bend your knees and squat slowly as you exhale. Stay at the bottom for a few minutes or as long as possible.

*Eka pada rajakapotasana* (**pigeon pose**) ～ Begin in a downward dog position, then lift your left leg and bring your knee towards your left wrist. Drop your knee on the mat and take your left foot towards your right wrist. Lower your whole body down to the floor then lift your chest and fold over the front (left) leg.

The calf of your front leg should be as close to a right angle with your body as possible (but it's fine if it's a little slanted). You can add a blanket under your front leg for more comfort or place a pillow or block under the hip if high and tilted. Stay here for a few minutes, taking deep breaths and then do the same on the other side.

# PREPARING FOR SLEEP

## Why sleep is so important

When we sleep, our cells regenerate, our muscles repair the wear and tear they have sustained throughout the day and our immune system replenishes itself. The cycle of day and night, of light and dark, is called the circadian rhythm and is essential to our health and well-being. However, it has become unbalanced in this 24-hour world, and we have forgotten the absolute need for darkness in our lives. It is at night that the hormone melatonin, our sleep hormone, is produced and its production can be severely reduced by bright light. Years ago, when our ancestors slept in the dark and arose with the rising sun, there was a natural rhythm to life, they were attuned to nature. It is only now that we have such imbalanced lifestyles, with constant stimulants like caffeine and alcohol, that we realize just how important the circadian rhythm really is.

## Time to go to sleep

According to Ayurveda, sleep is just as important as diet. The best time to sleep is from 10pm until 6am. These are the hours that are most rejuvenating and also our biorhythms are programmed to follow nature's rhythms, so ideally we should sleep when it's dark and wake with sunrise. Of course, seasonal changes affect these times, but 10pm is also a good time to sleep because of the dominance of the *kapha* element at this hour, making it more conducive to fall asleep.

## Winding down

We live in a fast-paced world. Many of us feel exhausted during the day but can't fall asleep at night, with constant thoughts, to-do lists and worries running through our minds. Naturally more of a night person, I often feel 'wired', with a sudden burst of energy, at night. It's hard to get to sleep when feeling energized or when the mind is pacing through thoughts. This is why there's now such an emphasis on winding down, on putting away your phone, on switching off from social media. It is important not just for the mind, but for all the body functions and our own wellbeing, to calm ourselves and activate our parasympathetic nervous system, so we're in 'rest and digest' mode (opposite to 'fight and flight'). Activation of our parasympathetic nervous system allows us to digest food properly, allows our muscles to relax and our heart rate to drop.

The realization of our absolute need to relax and de-stress is the reason why meditation apps are so widely used – they're as popular with the business and banking communities as they are with yogis. There have been a number of brilliant books on sleep in the last few years, from Arianna Huffington's *The Sleep Revolution* to *Why We Sleep: The New Science of Sleep and Dreams* by Matthew Walker. The world has woken up to the detrimental effects and consequences of insufficient sleep.

So how do we ensure that we can actually fall sleep? How do we create an environment that allows us to and encourages us to slow down and get into sleep mode at night?

**Environment** ❧ When you enter your home in the evening, lighting is the first thing that sets the tone and the mood. Bright lights can be stimulating, so try and have lights that dim or have a couple of lamps that you can use at night.

**Stimulants** ❧ What you've eaten during the day will, of course, have an impact on how well you sleep. If there is any caffeine in your system, it might prevent you from getting into that very deep sleep, so try not to have any coffee or anything with caffeine after around 3pm. Chocolate also contains caffeine. Having a small piece might be okay, but having a whole chocolate dessert or ice cream might affect your sleep.

**Turn off your phone** ✆ You may well find this difficult (like me) but try not to look at your phone for at least an hour before you sleep. The brightness of the screen and engagement with others on social media stimulates the senses and keeps everything 'on' rather than helping you to wind down in preparation for total switch off. When you go to bed, turn off your phone or don't take it into your bedroom. If you need to, switch on the alarm on your phone half an hour before you get into bed so that looking at your phone screen isn't the last thing you do before your head hits the pillow. Mobile phones are wonderful things but they can be disruptive for our sleep.

**Relaxation** ✆ What is it that relaxes you? For some, it might be playing a guitar and for others it will be listening to music while cooking. Do what relaxes you and brings you into a meditative state. All these things from cooking and listening to music to going for a walk to writing a journal or playing an instrument can be meditative, if it is what you love and enjoy. Schedule this time in, even if it feels selfish, because there will always be other things to do, people to meet, places to be, but if you never switch off from this, from the noise, from others, from the world, you will lose your connection to you and the essence of your own self.

**Stillness and meditation** ∿ For some, a meditation practice, whether it's long or short, can be incredibly therapeutic. I've expanded on this below and on the following pages with mantras to chant and different ways to get into a mode of stillness.

**Journalling and writing** ∿ Jotting down your thoughts can be a wonderful form of therapy and healing, making sense of all the fragmented thoughts and emotions, bringing them together in one place and finding a release.

**Soothing drinks** ∿ Sipping on hot milk with a little saffron and nutmeg can help induce sleepiness. Saffron not only helps you sleep but can even help with depression.

**Sesame oil** ∿ Rub sesame oil on the palms of your hands and bottoms of your feet – another Ayurvedic sleep remedy. You could also use ghee.

**Breathing** ∿ Taking deep breaths, or practising *ujjayi* breathing (see page 40), can be very calming and allow you to enter a state of relaxation. I often listen to podcasts by philosophers and thinkers or switch on my Indian classical playlist while I do my breathing exercises.

**Evening walk** ∿ Getting some fresh air, clearing the head and walking in the outdoors can be a wonderful way to de-stress. It might also be something you can do with your partner or a friend, a time to laugh and chat and re-energize the soul as you walk.

**Hot bath** ✎ Having a bath, perhaps with some candles, can be incredibly meditative and relaxing. For me, it's often just 10–15 minutes, but I put on some soothing music or an inspiring podcast, I light a candle, sip on a herbal tea or a cup of lemon, ginger and honey, and close my eyes.

Adding Epsom salts into your hot bath will additionally draw out toxins from the body, and Epsom salts also contain magnesium which enters the skin and muscles and helps us relax even more. This is great for when you've been lifting weights or just working out a lot. If you have a cold, then adding a little eucalyptus and camphor oil to your bath could be just the thing you need.

Baths are a wonderful way to send you into sleep mode before bed, but they're equally brilliant to warm the entire body in the winter, when you've just got home in the evening and it feels like the cold has penetrated into your bones. Try not to expose yourself to bright light after the bath so you stay in this relaxed state and get into bed as soon as possible after bathing.

**Steam and sauna** ✎ I love using a steam room and sauna especially in winter, first and foremost to warm up, and then to soothe any aches and pains and feel entirely relaxed. My skin also feels great after a short time in a steam room, because the sweating opens up the pores and helps to remove dead skin cells and toxins. In Ayurveda, the steam bath, called Swedana, increases circulation, helps remove toxins from fat cells, reduces stress (the heat and relaxation stimulate the release of endorphins), gives the heart a workout and helps clear sinuses.

**Evening playlist** ～ This eclectic collection of songs, for me, is infused with relaxed energy, mantras with upbeat rhythms to immediately bring the mind into evening mode and lift the mood, and with a sense of spiritual mystery.

'Hanuman Chalisa' – Keerti Mathur

'Mul Mantra' – Snatam Kaur

'Reunion' – Anoushka Shankar

'Morey Pya Bassey' – Cheb i Sabbah

'Bangles' – Niraj Chag

'Ong Namo' – Mirabai Ceiba

'Pashupati' – Sharon Gannon

'Nataraja' – Jai Uttal and Ben Leinbach

'Gayatri Mantra' – Deva Premal

'Hari Om (Tiruvannamalai)' – Janet Stone and DJ Drez

'Long Time Sun' – Snatam Kaur

'Purnamadah' – Shantala

'Jai Radha Madhav' – Deva Premal

'Water Sign' – East Forest

'Om Gam Ganapataye Namaha' – Edo & Jo

'I am (Krishan Liquid Mix)' – Nirinjan Kaur

'Rudrashtakam (Shiva Stuti)' – Krishna Das

## STILLNESS, SOUND AND PRAYER

The World Health Organisation labels stress as the health epidemic of the twenty-first century. The number of things we deal with on a daily basis, especially if we live in cities, is contributing to the rising levels of stress, from fast-paced jobs and busy social lives to the emotional stress of relationships or even the anxiety of missing out, exacerbated intensely by social media. This is why more and more people are turning to yoga, to meditation, understanding the importance of a quiet mind, of stillness, of scheduling time away from their phones and trying to instill a sense of relaxation and retreat in this beautiful yet frantic world.

In the evening, take a few minutes to gather and ground yourself, leaving all the flutter and fluster of the day to one side, letting it go for the night. You want to sleep with calmness, free from the energies and moods you've consumed and absorbed during the day. It is often this accumulation of thoughts and emotions that keeps us awake even if our bodies and minds are exhausted. Sit with your eyes closed and listen to your breath in the silence or to soft chanting or classical music, or repeat a mantra and do a mala.

## Healing with sound

When I studied Sanskrit in school, the alphabet was spoken with rhythm, beat and varying tones. We sung the stanzas from scriptures and there was musical intonation in everything. Sounds and music have vibrations known as *nada* in the Vedic tradition, sounds which can enhance wellbeing, boost mental health and even give a sense of spiritual awakening. Any sound that helps quieten the mind can be considered a healing sound. Closing the eyes and listening to the birds, the trees and leaves, listening to nature, can help calm us, can expand the mind and be incredibly healing.

Nada yoga is divided into external sounds – *ahata* – (music of nature, the birds, rain falling or sacred mantras) and internal sounds – *anahata* – (sounds felt through the heart *chakra*, closing your ears with your fingers and listening to your inner sounds).

Chanting (see pages 213–214) can raise and intensify the vibration of our whole being, body mind and spirit. Chanting should be full, opening the heart and the throat and being entirely immersed in it. It is a chant from the soul to the soul.

## Taking a sound bath

You might have heard about gong baths and crystal or Tibetan singing bowls. There's something truly magical about lying down and letting the vibrations of sounds from the gong instrument or crystal bowl wash over and through your body, thus a bath of sounds, to be absorbed into your consciousness and send you off into an effortless meditative state, sometimes even a deep sleep. Gong sound therapy and baths help reduce stress by activating the parasympathetic nervous system, the effects of which can last for days. The vibrations sink into your body and help your mind reach levels of meditation without 'trying' to – that's how I feel when I'm sleeping with the sounds of the gong reverberating in my ears. Rather like a shortcut to that space of stillness, of *shunyata*, within.

See the Resources section on page 247 for where to go for sound healing and gong baths.

## Mantra, *japa* and vibrations

Repetition of a mantra, called *japa,* calms the thoughts, gives the mind a focus and leads us to our inner self, our consciousness. The mantra is often the name of the divine, like *Rama*, or it is a universal word like *om* (the sound of the universe) or *sohum* (the sound of the breath). These sounds are a powerful way to align ourselves with the energy of the universe, and the internal vibration from the navel to the throat connects the physical body, the mind and the spiritual Self. The repetition of a mantra also activates the parasympathetic nervous system, by which the heart rate slows down and we therefore enter a state of relaxation.

*Japa* can be done with awareness and full concentration but can also be done in idle times when watching something or commuting. It gives you access to a constant uplifting force. Paramhansa Yogananda, Indian yogi, spiritual leader and founder of the organization Self-Realisation Fellowship explained that *japa* attunes the radio of our consciousness to positive, uplifting and God-reminding thought patterns. It spiritualises daily life.

Try if you can to chant these sounds and mantras out loud and observe the sounds vibrating in your own eardrums and in your body, feel the reverberations of those vibrations and sense the calming energy that seeps through the being during this time. If the mind wanders, let it, observe it, be aware of it, and bring it back to the mantra. Over time, the mind will be filled with a sense of emptiness. For simple mantras, see page 116.

## Using *mala* beads

Many people in India will have a *mala* or a *japa-mala*, a sacred garland rather like a rosary. It is used to aid *japa*, the recitation and repetition of a mantra. The *mala* is typically made from sacred woods like rudraksha or tulsi, which have their own significance and purpose; and traditionally a *mala* contains a certain number of beads strung together: a necklace typically has 108 beads (a *mala* worn around the wrist will have a smaller number), with one guru bead signalling the end of a full *japa* cycle.

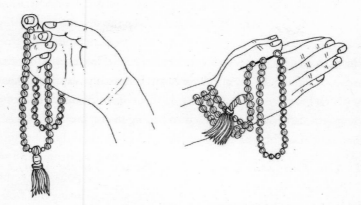

If your mind drifts, just let it and observe it, but be aware so that you can steer it back to the mantra or affirmation, rather like a meditation. Over time, this will happen more easily and naturally.

There are many reasons given for the number 108 – there are 108 *Upanishads* (sacred texts) and 108 marma or sacred energy lines in the body, points through which the *prana* flows, according to Ayurveda. The knots between each bead represent the connection of all beings.

Once you get in the rhythm of using the *mala* – it rests on the middle finger and the beads are rolled using the thumb – it will become automatic, something you do before you sleep, on your commute to work, even as you sit in a meeting. It will become a ritual that helps you focus, that strengthens your connection with the divine and with your own inner consciousness.

### Simple mantras to repeat

Here, I've put together some key mantras that have meaning to me, some of which you may have heard sung at a yoga class, some of which I have grown up reciting daily, all of which have a universal appeal and can be considered to belong to the spiritual, rather than religious, sphere.

ॐ **Aum, Om** ᐷ This is considered the sound of the universe, tuning into our connection with the universe and with nature, from which we have come.

The vibrations of this sound bring about steadiness of mind and slow down the nervous system. Symbolically the three syllables A-U-M are the sound of the creator, the preserver and the destroyer of the universe, the three characteristics and aspects of the Divine, connecting us with our own self and the *atman*, the higher self.

As you repeat this mantra with each breath, feel the energy lift from your pelvic floor all the way up to the crown of your head. The sound of *om* is also said to unblock the throat *chakra*, the *chakra* or energy field that controls communication.

सो हम् **Sohum** ᐷ a universal mantra meaning 'I am that', the understanding that I am the breath, I am connected to the universe, I am consciousness. The two syllables, *sooo* uttered on the inhale and *hum* on the exhale, are rather like the sound of our own breathing, creating a natural vibration, and through repetition, slowing the breath, deepening each breath and relaxing the nervous system.

राम **Rāma** ~ The name of Lord Rāma, the God who the epic scripture Ramayana is based upon, is considered to contain immense power. It is the mantra that Gandhi chose to chant and Rāma was, in fact, his last word. Aside from the wonderful stories of Rāma contained in the scripture, the word itself is made of 'ra', which represents the sun, 'a' representing *agni* or digestive fire and 'ma', the moon. These are the three sources of light on this earth and therefore repeating the name of Rāma is to also invoke light, the supreme light of the divine. Furthermore, Ra was the Sun God in ancient Egypt, and words like radiate and ray suggest an etymological origin. Delving further, the sun is the masculine or yang energy, which is radiated light, and the moon is the feminine or yin energy, which is reflected light, and thus the repetition of Rāma can help balance masculine and feminine energies within our being.

Other similar mantras, which you may have heard sung in temples or at gatherings, are *Hare Rama Hare Krishna*, praising and hailing both deities Rāma and Krishna, as well as *Shree Rama jai Rama jai jai Rama*, the repetition and singing of which has an almost trance-like effect.

**ॐ नमः शिवाय Om Namaḥ Shivaya** ॐ This is considered to be one of the most powerful mantras, in praise of Lord Shiva, but in fact a realization of inner Self. Shiva is known as the lord of destruction, but in fact this is the destruction of the *aham,* the 'I', the ego, after which only your inner Self is left, hence the inherent meaning of this mantra 'I bow to the inner Self'. The five syllables of this mantra are said to represent the five elements earth, water, fire, air and space, and their universal oneness; they symbolize universal consciousness.

**Gayatri mantra** ॐ

ॐ भूर्भुवः स्वः
तत्सवितुर्वरेण्यं
भर्गो देवस्य धीमहि
धियो यो नः प्रचोदयात् ॥

*oṃ  bhūr bhuvah svaḥ |*
*tat savitur varenyam*
*bhargo devasyadhīmahi |*
*dhiyo yo naḥ prachodayāt ||*

Let us meditate on the glory of the Almighty,
brilliant sun, the divine light and giver of life;
may he enlighten and inspire our mind.

The Gayatri mantra appeared in the Rig Veda, an early Vedic text written between 1800 and 1500 BCE. It is then mentioned in the

Upanishads as an important ritual and in the Bhagavad Gita as the poem of the Divine.

It is thought to be the most sacred phrase in the Vedas. The Gayatri mantra is also sung in a different way, so if you want to learn it, try and learn it by listening to it, either on Spotify or YouTube, and repeating each part. Once you've learned it, you'll be able to recite it in your mind while working, when walking, or even as a *japa* on your *mala*. While reciting the mantra, rather than contemplate its meaning, just listen to the sounds, feel the vibrations of those sounds and let them sink into your consciousness.

**Svasti mantra – Universal Peace Prayer** ∾ Humans have made religion divisive, but there is a unifying spiritual thread that runs through all religions. It is this force that connects us, a force akin to love that brings humanity together, a language that needs no explanation.

Prayer can be worship to a God, but it can also be a prayer for mankind, for humanity, for the divine within ourselves and in each of us. Here is one such Sanskrit prayer I learned as a child, that I've heard recited at spiritual gatherings in India and in yoga classes in London, a wonderful Sanskrit verse which speaks of love for all.

ॐ सर्वे भवन्तु सुखिनः
सर्वे सन्तु निरामयाः।

सर्वे भद्राणि पश्यन्तु
मा कश्चिद्दुःखभाग्भवेत् ।
ॐ शान्तिः शान्तिः शान्तिः ॥

*oṃ sarve bhavantu sukhinaḥ*
*sarve santu nirāmayāḥ*
*sarve bhadrāṇi paśyantu*
*mā kaściddduḥkhabhāgbhavet |*
*oṃ śāntiḥ śāntiḥ śāntiḥ ||*

May all be happy; may all be without disease
May all creatures have wellbeing
May none be in misery of any kind
May peace and peace and peace be everywhere.

**Lokah Samastah Sukhino Bhavantu** – wishing peace to all
beings ❧ Many yoga teachers use this mantra at the beginning
or the end of their practice, an invocation of collective peace.
The simplest translation of this mantra is 'Let the entire world
be happy.' It radiates compassionate concern and happiness for
others.

लोकाः समस्ताः सुखिनो भवंतु

**Shanti mantra** ❧ And lastly, this is the *Shanti* peace mantra from
Isha Upanishad, which contains the essence of the Upanishads,
that everything is perfect and whole, that nothing is less or insig-

nificant than the other, that we do not lack anything, but we are complete in ourselves.

ॐ पूर्णमदः पूर्णमिदं पूर्णात्पूर्णमुदच्यते ।
पूर्णस्य पूर्णमादाय पूर्णमेवावशिष्यते ॥
ॐ शान्तिः शान्तिः शान्तिः ॥

*om pūrnnamadah purnamidam pūrnaat pūrnāmudacyate*
*pūrnasya pūrnamādāya pūrnamevā vashissyate ||*
*om śāntiḥ śāntiḥ śāntiḥ ||*

That is whole; this is whole;
From whole comes whole;
If the whole is removed from the whole,
What remains is whole.
May peace and peace and peace be everywhere

## Moments of stillness

These short meditations are a few moments of stillness. It could be a few minutes or 15 minutes, or anything you like. The point is, even a few minutes of being still and being in a meditative state is a good starting point to let go and get ready for a calm sleep.

**Meditation 1 ~ Let it be and let it go** ❧ Find a moment of silence in the dark, light a candle if you can, sit upright, close your eyes and take a deep inhale. With this inhale, hold the breath, let the flurry of thoughts, whatever has happened today, anything that might or might not be bothering you, pass through your mind. And then, with the exhale, feel that collection of thoughts infiltrate out of you. Imagine the thoughts and worries and memories swim away like little fish in a gush of water. Visualize them trickling away from you. Take a few very deep breaths like this and each time, feel your mind empty again and again. With this sense of emptiness and letting go, allow your body to relax and let yourself settle into your yawn. Move your shoulders, arms or any part of your body that feels right. Press your fingers into your jaw and massage gently around the jaw line and the ears and feel yourself settle into sleep mode. This might be the right time to blow out the candle and get into bed.

**Meditation 2 ~ Gratitude** ᥫ Keep a little notepad for this because it's a wonderful thing to look back on. Every evening, take a few minutes to think about things that really brightened your day, the person who pronounced your name oddly when they gave you your coffee, making you laugh, the sun that peeked out from behind the clouds after days of grey weather, meeting a friend for lunch or having a random conversation with a stranger which made you smile. It could be absolutely anything. Gratitude is a practice that, once instilled, becomes a part of your life. You will start noticing things and be excited to note them down in the evening. During more difficult times, this practice will allow

### Become an observer of your emotions

As much as we live in the present and practise being mindful, memories sometimes pop up like hiccoughs, and with those memories come old emotions or new emotions, sometimes of loss or the sadness you felt at that time. It's great to have distractions, whether it's a social event we have to get to, friends to meet or a work deadline. It's also natural to talk to a friend or family, to use them as a way to bounce back and feel better. But once in a while, try to feel and observe the wave of emotion. Sit with it. Take a moment to feel the pain and acknowledge what you're thinking and feeling. Take long, deep breaths as you do this. Simply be, let yourself observe you, follow your thoughts and memories and see how that causes a shift in emotions. As the Indian sage Ramana Maharshi said, 'All that is required to realize the Self is to Be Still.'

you to find solace in those few moments, even if it is hard to think of them as something you're grateful for. Furthermore, you'll also start wanting to do things for others that will make *them* smile, whether it's a box of chocolates for your team at work or smiling at someone on the street, even if they deem it a little odd, or calling a friend you haven't spoken to in a while out of the blue. Again, the action could be anything at all, but the point is, you attract what you send out, you invite the kind of energy that you yourself radiate, so starting your own process of kind actions will gradually permeate your daily existence.

**Meditation 3 ~ Freedom of change** ⤚ Close your eyes and think about all the recent changes in your life. If there's one thing we know for certain it is that everything is always changing. Accepting this rather than resisting it will allow us to live happier lives. Take slow deep breaths as you let all these thoughts of changes swim around in your mind until they slow down and finally settle without agitation. Now reflect on change itself. This constant that will always be there. Can we find a little trust and faith that this change will always lead to something that is right for us? This acceptance of change gives you freedom in love – as Osho said 'Love is authentic only when it gives freedom.' Love comes into our life as a gift, but just as man himself has to die one day, just as a rose does not last forever, so also can love die. Feel these words, feel the changes that have happened in your life and feel the acceptance, or try to move your mind towards acceptance. With a few more very deep inhales, let the acceptance of this ever-changing life and world settle into you. You could also note down the changes in relationships and circumstances that you are resisting. Writing this down will enable you to understand exactly what it is that you're finding difficult to accept, it will help you to see it from another perspective and will allow you to fathom what to do about it or how to accept it. Now come back to stillness and close your eyes. If there is resistance in your mind, then just focus on the breath, focus on this moment right here, take a sound or mantra like *om* and chant it until you feel the sound settle the anxiety and thoughts.

## Taking a moment to appreciate your body

Some years ago, I was at a *kathak* (Indian classical dance) workshop with the legendary Indian dancer Pandit Birju Maharaj, and one particular thing he spoke about really stuck with me. He pulled his foot up and kissed it as he spoke playfully about his gratitude for his feet and what they're able to do. He might have even said that he kisses his feet every night. Having broken a bone in both feet over the last few years and then suffered a long two-month recovery each time, I have a heightened sense of appreciation for these two incredible things called feet that keep us grounded, allow us to walk, run, travel, go places, dance and simply move.

Of course, the hands and the feet are both such essentials, as is everything in our body, and the appreciation for any part of our body often dawns on us when we break or hurt something. It is so easy to forget this. Every now and again, when I'm getting into the shower, I suddenly remember those times when it wasn't so easy, when I would have to hop into the shower and balance. So, when you remember, smile inwardly and thank your body for the amazing things that it does every minute and every day. You could even do a quick meditation, closing your eyes, letting your attention and thoughts travel through each part of your body, observing the sensations in each part from your toes and fingertips to your collarbone and the crown of your head, ending with a quick thank you to this wonderful thing that we live in, our body.

# CONCLUSION

Ending the day with something positive, not taking stress to bed and being able to fall asleep and get a good night's sleep, is crucial to our entire wellbeing. Therefore, how we deal with distress, as well as how we de-stress, is imperative to carry us through the different passages of life. With many of us, it is only when we hit a wall, when we are faced with a life crisis, something that shakes us up, that we realize the need to make a change, the need to develop that muscle of inner strength and find our own tools for dealing with difficulties and healing from them. Understanding our need to recalibrate, to come home and unwind, will carry us through the next day with greater steadiness and can certainly help diffuse the impact of a crisis when it arrives.

# LIVING IS *MOKSHA*, LIBERATION

*Moksha*, liberation from the many lives for which our soul will return to this earth, is the ultimate aim of many Hindus. It is ending the cycle of birth, death and rebirth, so that the soul can be truly free. But what happens to the soul after that?

I rather like the idea that liberation can come, not with death, but while living on this earth, in moments of intense joy, in moments flowing with gratitude, in moments showered with grace, that bring tears to our eyes from overflowing bliss. It is the feeling of freedom and ecstasy as we live, when the clouds part and we see the golden hues in the blue sky.

This notion is akin to the *jivan-mukti* in ancient Indian philosophy, which means liberation from this life while living. Some choose the route of daily meditation to achieve self-realization, identifying the self and the soul as higher consciousness, while those on the path of *bhakti* (pure devotion and love) speak of finding this liberation through sheer ecstasy, loving God and living with passion. The ultimate purpose is the same, finding liberation and feeling a sense of the divine while living.

Rituals of wellbeing for the mind, body and soul keep us connected to our own self, to our own voice, to the soul within

us. As *our* world expands and connections increase, and simultaneously the world we are in becomes smaller as travel gets easier,
this sense of knowing who we are and being happy in our skin
seems more important than ever before. Our health is dependent
as much on a lack of disease as it is on feeling positive and happy.

### My inner Kailas

The clouds disperse in the morning, revealing the trembling
beauty of Mount Kailas, the abode of Lord Shiva, creator
and destroyer. I look up in awe at the spellbinding magnif-
icence of this mountain that is sacred to many faiths, but
that no human has ever been able to climb. Standing there,
meditating on this structure, fills and empties me, dispels
and creates, melts the heart and elevates the soul. It is silent,
the music of the river flowing by my side as though emerging
from this silence.

Mount Kailas breathes with magnetic energy, it is alive
with stories of Shiva and Shakti, it is shrouded in mystery.
The echoes of silence bounce off the snow-white padding and
this soundless vibration reverberates infinitely in my consciousness. The mountain, held on age-defying boulders that
warn us not to draw too close, sparkles in the golden sun.

Each time I gaze up, I feel that being in the presence of this mesmerizing being is like heaven. At night, Kailas glows and shines in the moonlight, the river glitters as it ripples over rocks, its calm melody filling the air. The nine days I am in Mount Kailas feel like another life, another world, an afterlife. And as I leave, as I look back on the last day, with the clouds closing in, about to swallow the entire mountain, my soul is consumed by a void, emptiness fills my heart, and I wonder how I will return to earth again.

Keep these moments close, moments that fill you with awe and inspiration and love, moments that connect you to the source, with nature, moments that fill your soul with spirit. And when you sit in *ekaant*, solitude, let your mind drift to that place where you once felt immense everlasting peace, where the fullness of silence consumed you and you felt momentary bliss that was beyond the realms of happiness. Here, you will find it again. You will find yourself.

The wisdom found in Ayurveda is thus bolstered by our understanding of life and our place in this world. Which is why health and philosophy go hand in hand.

And, as much as rituals, by name, are habitual repetitive actions or practices, it's just as important to inject the ritual of spontaneity now and again, something that surprises you, with a generous pinch of humour. For if there is one thing we can all be sure about on this planet, it is the ritual of change. And if there is one thing that will soften the pain and elevate the mood, it is humour – a shortcut to happiness.

# APPENDIX

## Ayurvedic herbs

Ayurveda prescribes spices, herbs and oils to calm the system, reduce inflammation and induce restfulness. When we were growing up, we would have to take *chyawanprash* with milk last thing at night. I remember dreading it. I would stand in the kitchen and gulp it down, trying not to taste it, rebelling by leaving a little on the spoon. Now, I choose to take it and, much to my surprise, I actually rather like the taste! *Chyawanprash* is a thick black paste or nutritive jam, a *churna*, containing over 25 Ayurvedic herbs and spices, all added to the main ingredient, the *amla* fruit (Indian gooseberry), a medicinal plant that is worshipped in India.

These potent herbs known as *rasayanas* have a wide variety of benefits. For example, if your mind is very active at night and you

have insomnia, *brahmi* and *ashwagandha* could help, alongside creating a calm environment to relax in before you sleep, perhaps having a bath and eating early. Taking a sleeping pill might seem like an easy option, but it doesn't deal with the causes of insomnia. For one person, lack of sleep might be down to overeating, eating the wrong foods in the evening or eating too late; whereas for another, it could be a stressful job, which affects their mind even after working hours.

There are other Ayurvedic herbs you can take for boosting cognitive ability, for digestion, insomnia, to regulate blood sugar, for the joints and more. Here's a shortlist of some of the most powerful Ayurvedic herbs and what they can do. It is best to consult an Ayurvedic practitioner before deciding which to take as there are some contraindications for the herbs, but generally speaking, anyone can take the popular *chyawanprash*.

**Amla** ⌒ One of the herbs in triphala, amla is also used on its own for rejuvenation, for its high vitamin C content and to boost immunity. It is the small Indian gooseberry, a round and very sour fruit, easy to juice or to take in tablet form. It is high in antioxidants, can help with colds or flu and balances the *doshas*. It is one of the key ingredients in *chyawanprash* paste, a jam-like mixture of vital herbs that is believed to boost body strength and the immune system, kindle the *agni* (digestive fire) and build *ojas* (see page 19). Amalaka, one of the Sanskrit names for this small tree, translates as 'The Sustainer'. This tree is mentioned in the

Upanishads. There are beautiful stories of how it came about from the gods; it is a tree that is worshipped on the day of Shivratri, when red and yellow threads are tied around its trunk. The Indian gooseberry is sacred, for it is associated with fertility. You can read more about it in *Sacred Plants of India* by Nanditha Krishna and M. Amirthalingam.

**Ashwagandha** 〜 This is one of the most powerful herbs in Ayurvedic healing. It's used for a variety of conditions. It helps with anxiety and stress, can help strengthen the immune system after illness or surgery, helps calm inflammation in the joints, lowers blood sugar, lowers the stress hormone cortisol and enhances testosterone.

**Brahmi** 〜 Brahmi is a brilliant brain tonic, it improves cognitive ability, is known to reduce the stress hormone cortisol and helps to regulate the hormones involved with the stress response. Furthermore, by increasing the hormone serotonin, it can also decrease anxiety.

**Neem** 〜 The leaves of a neem tree are a remedy for skin infections, spots and scars. Neem is a very powerful blood purifier and neem oil helps with muscle and joint pain. The neem tree, in fact, expels more oxygen than other trees and therefore purifies the air. The neem tree is called 'symbol of truth' and is often worshipped in places where there is no temple and given the same offerings as the gods. Some Indians hang neem leaves at the entrance of their house when a child is born to keep out infections, and in other places, like Tamil Nadu and Andhra Pradesh, people perform the wedding of the pipal tree and the neem tree as a fertility rite to invoke rain; both are linked and are known to grow together.

**Triphala** ᴠ This is a classic Ayurvedic combination of three Indian herbs (*haritaki*, *bahera* and *amlaki*) which helps digestion, strengthens the digestive system and helps good bacteria to flourish in the gut. The combination of the three herbs helps balance all the *doshas*, as each of the herbs or fruits balances one *dosha*, therefore working on the constitution of the body as a whole. Amlaki or amla, the Indian gooseberry, also helps lower cholesterol and is rich in vitamin C. Ayurveda suggests taking triphala in a pill form at night just before you sleep.

## Home remedies and treatments

When I was growing up, my mother and grandmother would concoct home remedies for everything from sniffles and colds to cuts and spots. For colds, I was given turmeric milk or a spoonful of a honey and turmeric paste, and now I think of turmeric as a preventative agent, to be taken daily. These remedies have been handed down from generation to generation. No one really knows where this wisdom originated but much of it has its roots in Ayurveda, coupled with a good deal of trial and error over thousands of years. Most of these remedies are herbal or plant-based.

Of course, these remedies may, in some cases, only provide quick temporary relief if more permanent diet and lifestyle changes are needed, or if the issue really requires medicine. For example, if you are trying a herbal remedy and taking ginger, honey, lemon and turmeric a few days after your cold has turned into an infection and reached your lungs, the spices may help but you might need antibiotics, whereas taken at the very start, when your cold was just a cold, it would have helped a lot more.

So, if the problem isn't chronic and could perhaps be solved or eased by using herbal home remedies or spices, then it's worth trying a few of these and finding which one works for you. It is important to remember that every single person's constitution is different and that you will benefit from doing your own research. Start off with small doses if you know your body is sensitive. It is also important to understand that a little of everything can be good, but too much of even the healthiest food can be detrimental. For example, all nuts are rich in nutrients and vitamins, but they need to be chewed well because they can be difficult to digest, and more than a handful of nuts can easily bloat you and be too heavy on the stomach.

**Acidity** ⮞ Chew a whole clove after your meal if you get acidity after eating. You can also sip on a glass of water with a piece of jaggery (see page 181) dissolved in it after meals.

**Breastfeeding** ⮞ Millet flour helps to increase milk supply and contains minerals that are good for mother and baby. *Raab* is a thick drink made from millet cooked in ghee and ajwain (carom) seeds, with sweet mineral-rich jaggery (see page 180 for the recipe). Each component is beneficial to both mother and baby and it can be drunk a few times a day while breastfeeding.

*Goondh*, made from a tree bark resin, is known to support recovery following childbirth and provides vital nutrients. *Katlu*, a healthy granola-style sweet snack containing *goondh* and other nourishing ingredients, is often given to new and expectant mothers in India.

**Blood sugar and digestion** ⮞ Soak ¼–½ a teaspoon of fenugreek seeds in water overnight night, drink the water in the morning and chew the seeds. This is a great natural medicine for everything from digestion, blood sugar and diabetes to blood pressure and arthritis.

**Clear eyes and skin** ⮞ My mum used to soak five unblanched almonds overnight, and we would peel the skin in the morning before eating them. Eating a few soaked almonds in the morning is a good habit to form. Having them with raisins and a glass of milk can make for a perfect light breakfast. Soaking nuts makes them easier to digest, but chew them really well. If you are low in iron, soak the almonds overnight, and in the morning blend them with milk and jaggery (see page 181) to make a nutritious, iron-rich drink.

**Colds and congestion** ❧ Turmeric and ginger are both anti-inflammatory, healing and wonderful as preventative measures, and to have when you have a cold or flu, but they may not be an effective cure if your cold has become more of an infection. It will certainly help regardless of whether you are taking medication or not.

— Mix together 1 teaspoon of ground ginger, 1 teaspoon of ground turmeric, 1 tablespoon of honey and eat. Decrease the amount of ginger for children as it might be too spicy.

— Turmeric in hot milk at night especially, but this can be had at any time.

— Lemon or lime juice with ginger juice can be taken as a shot or could be stirred into hot water.

— Boil grated fresh ginger and fresh turmeric in water for 10 minutes. Pour into a mug, then squeeze in half a lemon and stir in 1 teaspoon of honey. Grating releases more juice than simply slicing. If you don't have fresh ginger and turmeric root, just stir some ground ginger and ground turmeric into a mug of hot water.

— If you can manage the spiciness, then have a small shot of mixed pure ginger and turmeric juices. Add honey if you need to.

**Cough** ᔎ If you have fits of dry coughing, suck a few black peppercorns or suck a whole clove.

— **Tulsi leaves:** the leaves of the holy basil or tulsi plant can help clear the respiratory passages and can also help bring down a temperature. Boil these leaves in hot water with peppercorns and cloves or just by themselves.

**Cuts** ᔎ If you have a cut and it's bleeding, applying ground turmeric will help stop the bleeding and will speed up the healing process. You could fill the cut with ground turmeric and then apply a plaster to ensure the turmeric stays there and doesn't stain your clothes.

**Flatulence and bloating** ᔎ Discomfort or bloating in the stomach after a meal can be caused by undigested foods, foods that perhaps don't suit our constitution or perhaps how much we ate. There are various things you can do to help ease that feeling.

— Ground ginger in a mug of hot water is great on its own, but adding a little *hing* (asafoetida) to it and a pinch of Himalayan salt (optional), makes it more potent and effective for bloating. Asafoetida is the strong and bitter powder that is added to certain curries and dals to give extra flavour, but it also has anti-flatulent, anti-inflammatory and antiseptic properties which counterbalance things like beans and lentils.

— Another concoction is jaggery (see page 181), asafoetida and black pepper in warm water.

— Add mint leaves to hot water, let this cool down, then drink. Or add a drop of peppermint essential oil to water.

— For a daily digestion aid, boil cumin seeds, fennel seeds and ajwain (carom) seeds in water, or add them to your mug of hot water and sip on this. You can also let the water cool down, then fill up your water bottle and sip on this throughout the day.

**Flaky and itchy scalp** ❧ I've always struggled with a dry scalp and the only thing that really works for me is coconut oil. Massage it into the scalp the night before washing your hair or even just an hour or two before washing it. It also helps to condition the scalp and the massage stimulates the hair follicles and therefore can help with hair growth.

**High cholesterol** ❧ Raw garlic can help reduce cholesterol. Chop a clove of garlic into small pieces, and swallow a teaspoon of the garlic with a whole glass of water so that you can't taste it. You could try having this in the morning before breakfast to mask the taste of garlic. Onion juice also helps reduce cholesterol.

**Indigestion** ❧ Chew ½ teaspoon of ajwain (carom) seeds with a pinch of salt. If you find these seeds spicy, swallow them with a glass of water. They should almost instantly settle the stomach. A super simple and effective way to combat indigestion.

**Insomnia** ❧ Milk with a pinch of saffron strands, plus grated nutmeg for more potency. (See pages 205–210 for other sleep aids.)

**Make-up removal** ❧ Eye make-up is the hardest make-up to remove. Nothing beats coconut oil at removing all that liner and mascara. I usually put a few drops on the tips of my fingers and massage my eyes until it feels like all the liner and mascara has thinned. I then wash my face with my usual face wash and warm water. My eye make-up washes off so easily like this.

**Pick-me-up** ❧ Whenever you need a pick-me-up in the morning or at night, spray your face with rose water. Leave it in the fridge in the summer in a spray bottle.

**Sore throat** ✺ If you wake up with a sore throat or even if you feel a little tingling, gargle half a glass of warm water with a teaspoon of salt. You can also do this throughout the day, but certainly starting the morning with this will ease the soreness in the throat.

Another option is to boil a teaspoon of ajwain (carom) seeds in a few cups of water, then strain, add ½ teaspoon of salt and gargle this twice a day.

**Swollen face** ✺ Performing a *shirshasana* (headstand) reverses the flow of gravity and flushes your face with oxygen, which is great for the face and skin. It also increases blood flow to the scalp, which improves hair growth. If you can't do a headstand, a shoulder stand will do the trick! Another quick trick I use is to soak a face towel in water, wring it out and then place in the fridge overnight. In the morning, cover the face with the cold towel and rest for a few minutes. It helps to calm any swelling (especially if you've been on a plane the day before).

**Toothache** ✺ Cloves contain a chemical called eugenol, which acts as an anesthetic and antibacterial agent. Cloves have been used in both Indian and Chinese medicine to relieve pain. You can either place a whole clove where you have tooth pain for a few minutes at a time or dip a tissue or cotton ball into clove oil and dab it over the gums in the area of pain. The eugenol in cloves is also known to fight oral bacteria.

**Travel sickness** ❧ Keep a whole clove under the tongue and suck on this as you travel. It will help calm any feeling of nausea.

**Vomiting and nausea** ❧ Stir ¼ teaspoon of sugar, ¼ teaspoon of salt and a pinch of ground black pepper into a mug of hot water, and just before drinking, stir in a pinch of bicarbonate of soda.

This can help stop vomiting, as well as help with nausea and upset stomachs.

# RESOURCES AND RECOMMENDATIONS

## Holistic, medical and bodywork therapists in London

On my journey to my own health and wellbeing, I've worked with the following practitioners and found them to be powerful, healing and transformational. Please check my website for updates on practitioners and events: www.miramanek.com

### Dr M. Ali – marma therapy and integrative approach

Integrated Medical Centre, Marylebone

For a holistic all-round consultation, effective marma treatment and integrative medicine and bodywork. Dr Ali works with elements of Ayurveda, Chinese medicine and the European system from Hippocrates, along with herbs, yoga and self-healing, and is able to help many conditions and diseases.

www.drmali.com

www.integratedmed.co.uk

### Dr Wei Wu – bodywork, realignment and integrative approach

Intuitive intelligent bodywork using Chinese medicine, correcting the body with origin point medicine, working on alignment through the pelvis and giving lifestyle and dietary solutions to reduce inflammation in the body.

www.weiwuwellness.com

### Kate Siraj – Ayurveda

Kate Siraj is the founder of The Ayurveda Practice. She has a wealth of knowledge, consults on lifestyle and food and does Ayurvedic therapies.

www.ayurvedapractice.com

### Jono Condous – Ayurveda

Jono also consults from Triyoga Chelsea and Triyoga Camden on certain days.

www.ayurvedabrighton.co.uk

### Rebecca Dennis – transformative breathwork

Rebecca Dennis runs one-to-one breathwork sessions at Indaba Yoga in Marylebone. Through a guided session of intense breathwork, Rebecca allows you to connect to the power of your breath and through that to your emotions and headspace. You might go through crying, laughing, numbness and some dizziness from all the breathing. But it's truly transformational. Thereafter, join one of her group sessions.

www.breathingtree.co.uk

### Other transformative breathwork classes:

I love going for kundalini yoga classes and for prana kriya yoga, both of which use intense breath to build energy, move the *prana* and awaken the hidden energy of the kundalini. Yogi Ashokananda has prana kriya yoga and meditation classes and courses all over London including at Triyoga. My favourite kundalini classes are Carolyn Cowan and Sivaroshan, both at Triyoga.

www.yogiashokananda.com

www.carolyncowan.com

www.sivaroshan.co.uk

## Gong baths and sound bowl healing

These have become very popular recently. Many yoga studios offer sound baths, and there are now studios dedicated to sound bowl healing, breathwork and meditation such as Re:mind Studio (www.remindstudio.com) in London's Eccleston Yards and Lifespace in Notting Hill (www.lifespacehealing.com). Leo Cosendai, London's foremost sound healer, has also launched the Third Space app and does teacher training (www.leocosendai.com).

# Ayurveda resources and study

## Ayurvedic Professionals Association

To find a practitioner and information about Ayurveda in the UK, visit www.apa.uk.com

## The College of Ayurveda, Milton Keynes

www.ayurvedacollege.org

## Holistic Centres in the UK

### The Kailash Centre

St John's Wood, London

Offering a range of holistic treatments from Ayurvedic medicine and acupuncture to Tibetan medicine and Chinese medicine.

www.kailashcentre.org

### Triyoga – yoga, therapy, food

Soho, Camden, Chelsea, Shoreditch, Ealing, London

Variety of yoga classes, workshops and teacher training, as well as a plethora of holistic therapists across all centres.

www.triyoga.co.uk

### Re:Mind Studio

Eccleston Yards, London

London's first boutique meditation studio offering drop-in meditation classes from gong meditation and crystal bowl healing to reiki and yin yoga.

### The Clover Mill

Malvern, Worcestershire

A boutique Ayurvedic spa retreat with various residential workshops.

www.theclovermill.com

**Essential Ayurveda**

Halton Holegate, Spilsby, Lincolnshire

A residential retreat with Ayurvedic treatments and products with various cookery and yoga workshops.

www.essentialayurveda.co.uk

**Ayurveda Pura**

North Greenwich, London

Offering a whole range of Ayurvedic treatments, Ayurvedic courses, Ayurvedic herbs, holistic creams and spa equipment as well as an Ayurvedic café.

www.ayurvedapura.com

## Ayurvedic resorts and holistic centres in India

Ishavilas, Goa (developed by Dr Ali, UK – see page 245)
    www.ishavilasgoa.com
Carnoustie, Kerala
    www.carnoustieresorts.com
Vaidyagrama, Coimbatore, Tamil Nadu
    www.vaidyagrama.com
Ayurveda Yoga Villa, Kerala
    www.ayurvedayogavilla.com
Devaaya, Goa
    www.devaaya.com

Somatheeram, Kerala
       www.somatheeram.org/en
Atmantan, Pune
       www.atmantan.com
Kare Ayurveda & Yoga Retreat, Pune
       www.karehealth.com
Ananda Spa, Himalayas
       www.anandaspa.com

## My favourite podcasts

Podcasts are a great way of learning more while walking or travelling, they're a source of inspiration, providing food for thought and some great 'aha' moments. They're an easy and accessible way to digest interesting information on whatever topic interests you.

Alan Watts podcast – or on YouTube
Oprah's *Super Soul Conversations by Oprah*
Deepak Chopra's *Infinite Potential*
*The Cabral Concept* by Stephen Cabral
*Good Life Project* by Jonathan Fields
*Feel Better Live More* by Dr Rangan Chatterjee
*Everyday Ayurveda* by Myra Lewin
*Under the Skin* with Russell Brand
*The Ghee Spot* by Katie Silcox
*On Purpose with Jay Shetty*, by Jay Shetty

## Useful Books

*Aim True* by Kathryn Budig

*Absolute Beauty, Radiant Skin and Inner Harmony*, by
　　　Pratima Raichur with Marian Cohn

*Perfect Health* by Deepak Chopra

*Too Young to Grow Old* by Anne-Lise Miller

*The Ayurvedic Cookbook* by Amadea Morningstar with
　　　Urmila Desai

*East by West* by Jasmine Hemsley

*Waste Not* by Erin Rhoads

*Shinrin-Yoku, The Art and Science of Forest-Bathing* by
　　　Dr Qing Li

*The Power of Silence* by Graham Turner

*Autobiography of a Yogi* by Paramhansa Yogananda

*You Can Heal Your Life* by Louise Hay

*Gene Eating* by Giles Yeo

*The 4 Pillar Plan* and *The Stress Solution* by Dr Rangan
　　　Chatterjee

# Acknowledgements

This book has brought together all that I love, breathe and live. The research and writing has felt like the final part of a process of transformation in my life, a culmination of the stories and strands that together weave my journey to where I am now. The seed of *Prajñā* was, in fact, sown by my agent Stuart Cooper – thank you for believing I could write this book!

I started writing my initial thoughts on paper on the beaches of Goa, in between sunset swims, yoga mornings and watching the moon rise in the sky. It took a whole year to formulate and structure this concept into a book proposal in a way that made philosophical concepts and an Ayurvedic way of living accessible to the reader.

Thank you to my editor Anna Steadman for choosing to publish *Prajñā* and for helping me bring the concept to life and to Jessica Farrugia for helping to get the book and the message out into the world. Thank you to Dr M. Ali for sharing your knowledge, to Kate Siraj, Alicia Roscoe and Faraaz Tanveer for answering all my questions. Thank you to my sister Meenal Sachdev for reading through and helping me with the passages on philosophy, and to my mother Hema Manek for assisting me with testing all the recipes.

# Index